John Ward

Round and through the Wesleyan hymn book

John Ward

Round and through the Wesleyan hymn book

ISBN/EAN: 9783742840806

Manufactured in Europe, USA, Canada, Australia, Japa

Cover: Foto ©Thomas Meinert / pixelio.de

Manufactured and distributed by brebook publishing software
(www.brebook.com)

John Ward

Round and through the Wesleyan hymn book

ROUND AND THROUGH

THE

WESLEYAN HYMN BOOK.

BY THE

REV. J. WARD.

O COME, GLAD PRAISES SING
TO THE EVERLASTING KING;
SING TO THE LORD, AND SHOUT WITH GLAD ACCLAIM!
FOR GOODLY 'TIS AND SWEET,
OUR GOD WITH PRAISE TO GREET;
AND PRAISES WELL BEFIT THE ALMIGHTY NAME.

MANT.

LEEDS :

PRINTED BY B. W. SHARP, BRIGGATE.

MDCCCLXVIII.

PREFACE.

THE Writer of the following pages has long thought that a cheap little hand-book comprising information on the rise, formation, authorship, and other historical particulars connected with the Wesleyan Hymn Book, was greatly needed by the masses in Methodism. It is an admitted fact that the Methodist people generally know but very little about a book which they greatly love, and which is in constant use amongst them. Tens of thousands of them have no other idea but that John Wesley wrote all the hymns, whereas only about five or six of them are known to have been written by him, along with twenty-six translations. Others have supposed them to be the joint productions of Messrs. John and Charles Wesley, whilst in fact a hundred and fifteen are from the pens of other authors, of which number ten belong to Dr. Doddridge, and sixty-six to Dr. Watts.

The writer is not unmindful of the existence of such works as Burgess' Hymnology; Kirk's Original Titles; Heaton's Lectures; Christopher's Hymns and Hymn Writers: yet, valuable and interesting as these all are, they do not realize what is required by the individuals just alluded to,—the humbler classes of our people. Not only are some of them too expensive and elaborate, but wanting also in adaptation to the class of readers we have named.

The design of this hand-book is to help such persons to a more profitable use of our incomparable hymns, as well as a more intelligent and devout appreciation of their worth. No attempt has been made to criticise the literary merits of the Hymn Book, or to alter or amend any of its contents; such an effort would be altogether apart from the object sought to be attained, which is simply and solely to assist the humbler portion of the Methodist people to understand the circumstances which placed in their possession a book, which, next to the Bible, they love and prize above all others; a book which has refreshed and cheered, by its inspiring strains, many a weary way-worn christian.

If this production should in any measure tend to interest and profit God's people, the writer will feel compensated for his toil, and will rejoice that he has been the means of elevating in their esteem those precious hymns, compared with which, "Italian trills are tame."

In working out this design he purposes, according to the title, to go ROUND the Hymn Book by sketching its history, and THROUGH it by describing its contents. And may the blessing of God rest upon the endeavour.

Round and Through

THE WESLEYAN HYMN BOOK.

SINGING is an exercise in which the heart of man finds a ready and joyous utterance. The power of song is felt and acknowledged by all people. "The man that makes the ballads of a nation," says a celebrated writer, "need not care who should make its laws." If, as has been often said, friendship is the "wine of life," and variety is the "spice of life," so singing is the "charm of life," as one of the poets has truly said,—

> "Of all the arts beneath the heaven,
> That man hath found, or God hath given,
> None bears the human soul away,
> Like the sweet strains of melody."

Like many other good things, singing has been greatly abused and turned to the most unworthy purposes. Whilst angels use it to pour forth their adorations, the sons of belial employ it in carnal revelry and bacchanalian strains.

When the great Creator of all things fastened the foundations of the earth, and laid the corner stone thereof, the heavens became vocal with His praise, "the morning stars sang together, and all the sons of God shouted for joy." One of the most rapturous and inspiring representations of the heavenly world is that which sets forth the songs of the redeemed. Saint John beheld in apocalyptic vision, the glorified hosts standing on a sea of glass, having the harps of God in their hands, whilst they "sing the song of Moses the servant of God, and the song of the Lamb." In the temple worship of the Jews singing formed a distinguished part of their devotions, and all the world is invited to join them in this high and holy service in the following words, "Make a joyful noise before Him all ye lands, serve the Lord with gladness, and come before His presence with singing. Enter into His gates with thanksgiving, and into His courts with praise, be thankful unto Him, and bless His Name." The christian church has not been unmindful of its benefits, but has in various ways consecrated her sweetest and sublimest strains to the worship of God and the service of religion. In the earliest period of the church's history we find singing not only practised and tolerated, but positively enjoined. When our Lord and His disciples partook of the first eucharistic feast they closed the service with a hymn of praise. "And when they had sung an hymn, they went out into the mount of Olives." In the prison at Philippi, Paul and Silas sang praises to God at midnight. One of the apostolic injunctions was, " Let the word of Christ dwell in you richly, in all wisdom, teaching and admonishing one another in psalms, and hymns, and spiritual songs, singing with grace in your hearts to the Lord." St. James says, "Is any among you afflicted ? let him pray. Is any merry ? let him sing psalms." Singing is in perfect harmony with the genius and spirit of the christian religion. An eloquent writer has said, " To other and higher distinctions of christianity as a system of worship must be added that it is pre-eminently the lyrical religion of the world. Discord and silence divide all others between them. But the christian sings. To him this is so natural, and, indeed, so necessary an act as to be quite beyond the range of sanction and apology. Indeed, apart from all precedent, a faith which is itself the harmoniser of the discordant elements of life can have no other than a tuneful utterance."

The practice of singing hymns and psalms was continued in the church immediately succeeding the Apostolic age. Pliny, a Roman historian, who flourished at the end of the first century, in a letter which he addressed to the emperor Trajan, describes the christians as " assembling together before daylight, and singing a hymn of praise to Christ as God." Tertullian, one of the christian fathers, who lived in the latter part of the second century, when speaking of the manner in which the Lord's supper was administered, says, " After water is brought for the hands, and lights, we are invited to sing to God according as each one can propose a subject from holy scripture, or his own composing." Saint Augustine, who flourished about the end of the third century, describes the influence of christian psalmody in his day. He says, " The hymns of the church moved my soul intensely; the truth was distilled by them into my heart; the flame of piety was kindled, and my tears flowed for joy.

Singing has formed a part of public worship, with very few exceptions, in every age of the church, and in every portion of the world where the christian religion has been established. In the Romish church, however, the psalms and hymns were chanted only by the appointed choirs, whilst the congregation took no part therein. But when the glorious Reformation broke the yoke of popery from the necks of British christians, one of the first-fruits of that great deliverance was the privilege of conducting divine worship in the common language of the people, and of all the congregation joining together to praise God in His temple. Strype, the annalist, refers to the first exercise of the right in this country. He says, " In the month of September began the new morning prayer at St. Antholin's, London, the bell beginning to ring at five, when a psalm was sung after the Geneva fashion, all the congregation, men, women, and boys singing together." Bishop Jewel, when writing to Peter Martyr in 1560, says, " Religion is now somewhat more established than it was· The

people are everywhere exceedingly inclined to
the better part. The practice of joining in
church music has very much conduced to this.
For as soon as they had commenced in public
in one little church in London, immediately not
only in the churches in the neighbourhood, but
even the towns far distant began to vie with
each other in the practice. You may now see
sometimes at St. Paul's Cross, after the service,
six thousand persons, old and young, of both
sexes, all singing together and praising God.
This sadly annoys the mass priests and the
devil, for they perceive by this means the
sacred discourses sink more deeply into the
minds of men, and that their kingdom is weak-
ened and shaken at almost every note."

Luther, the great reformer, was most diligent
in providing for the newly reformed churches
means and facilities for celebrating the praises
of God in public worship. "Amongst other
steps taken by him in support of the revival of
true religion, he listened to the wishes of the
congregation to recover that share in their
church songs of which their Latin guides had
deprived them. Accordingly, he collected all
the old hymns he could find, selected the most

beautiful, altered whatever tended to superstition and error, and used them in the public and private worship of God. He himself also added to the stock. Gifted with high feelings, profound learning and piety, natural taste, and an enthusiastic and poetic imagination, he composed very many pieces hitherto unsurpassed as religious lyrics. With the airs he proceeded in the same way. Old melodies, sacred and profane, he incessantly collected from every quarter, from pilgrimage songs, and minnesingers' chants, from cloisters and from markets, from wandering minstrels and from begging friars, arranged their sweet notes to his precious words, and thus restored the most beautiful to public worship."

In our own country very little was done to promote this branch of divine worship until a considerable period after the Reformation. Several attempts were made by different individuals. Miles Coverdale, bishop of Exeter, published a volume of psalms and hymns, and acquired the designation of "the father of metrical psalmody." The following quaint apostrophe appears upon the title-page of his book.

Go lytel boke get the acquaintaunce,
Among the lovers of God's worde :
Gev them occasyon the same to avaunce ;
And to make their songes of the Lord,
That they may thrust under the borde,
All other ballettes of fylthyness ;
And that we all with one accorde,
May gev ensample of godlyness.

Go little boke among men's children,
And get thee to their companye ;
Teach them to sing the commaundements ten,
And other ballettes of God's glorye.
Be not ashamed, I warrande thee,
Though thou be rude in songe and ryme,
Thou shalt to youth some occasion be,
In godlye sportes to pass they'r tyme.

In 1549, Sternhold's Book of Psalms in metre, was first published, and bore the following title : "*All such Psalms of David as Thomas Sternholde, late Groome of the Kynge's Majestye's Robes did in his lyfetime drawe into Englyshe Metre.*"* To these were added fifty more by Hopkins and others, and in its complete form it bore the following inscription, modernised—

---

* About a year before this date Sternhold published the first edition of his Psalms, consisting of nineteen, one copy only of which is known to exist.

" The whole Book of Psalms collected into
English Metre, by Thomas Sternhold, John
Hopkins, and others, conferred with the Hebrew, with apt notes to sing them withal. Set
forth and allowed to be sung in all churches, of
all the people together, before and after morning and evening prayers, and also before and
after sermon, and moreover in private houses,
for their godly solace and comfort, laying apart
all ungodly songs and ballads which tend only
to the nourishing of vice and corrupting of
youth." The following clause is found amongst
the Injunctions of Queen Elizabeth to the
Clergy, A.D., 1559 : " For the comforting of
such that delight in Music, it may be permitted
that at the beginning or end of Common
Prayer, either at Morning or Evening, there
may be sung an Hymn, or such like song, to
the praise of Almighty God, in the best Melody
or Music, that may be conveniently devised,
having respect that the sense of the Hymn
may be understood and perceived." In 1553
an attempt was made to versify the Acts of the
Apostles by one Doctor Tye, whose book was
sent forth under the following lengthy title :
" *The Acts of the Apostles, translated into En-*

lyshe Metre, and dedicated to the Kinge's most excellent Majestye, by Christofer Tye, Docter in Musyke, and one of the Gentylemen of hys Graces most honourable Chappell, with Notes to eache Chapter to synge and also to play upon the Lute; very necessarye for Students after their Studye to fyle theyr Wyttes, and also for all Christians that cannot synge, to read the good and godlye Storyes of the Lives of Christ and his Apostles." We give a specimen verse or two of the Doctor's composition on the 14th chapter, 1st verse.

> It chaunced in Iconium,
> As they oftimes did use,
> Together they into dyd cam,
> The Sinagoge of Jues.
>
> When they dyd preache and onlye seke
> God's grace then to atcheve,
> That they so spake to Jue and Greeke,
> That many dyd beleve.

Others tried their hands at writing hymns, or putting into metre the Book of Psalms, some of whom were persons of distinction, including bishops, statesmen, heroes, and even kings. Henry the Eighth, that paragon of sanctity and sensuality, ventured to give the world some of his effusions. The following evening hymn of his, containing some very devotional sentiments, is still in existence,—

> O Lorde, the Maker of all thing!
> We pray Thee now in this evening,
> Us to defend through Thy mercy,
> From all deciete of our enemy.
> Let neither us deluded be,
> Good Lorde, with dream or phantasy;
> Our hearte wakyng in The, Thou Keepe,
> That we in sinne fall not on sleepe.
> O, Father, through Thy blessed Sonne,
> Grant us this our petition,
> In whome, with the Holy Ghost alwaies,
> In heaven and earth be laude and praise. Amen.

It was not until the beginning of the last century that British Hymnology received its birth in the productions of the devout and learned Doctor Watts. Possessed largely of a devotional spirit, and endowed with rich poetic gifts, he struck out a path peculiarly his own, and in that path he wrought a work which has immortalized his name. Whether he is entitled to the high distinction which many have assigned him as the "first great hymnist in the world," we are not prepared to decide; but, unquestionably, he deserves the honour of being considered the first great reformer of Christian Psalmody in this country; and is worthy of being called, what he has been often designated, "The Poet of the Sanctuary." The first edition of his hymns was published, in 1707.

The eighteenth century was remarkable for the numerous hymn writers which it produced, amongst whom were the four Wesleys, Watts, Doddridge, Hart, Cowper, Newton, Cennick, Toplady, and Beddome. Some of the most popular and favorite hymns were published about the same time; such as, "Come Thou fount of every blessing," by Robinson; "All hail the power of Jesu's Name," by Edward Perronett; "Ashamed of Jesus," etc., by Joseph Grigg; "How tedious and tasteless the hours," by John Newton; and, "Guide me, O Thou great Jehovah," by Williams, a Welsh clergyman.

An interesting circumstance is said to have taken place in connection with Robinson and the hymn just named, for the correctness of which we do not vouch. He was first a popular minister among the Calvinistic Methodists, and afterwards became a celebrated preacher in the Baptist community, but ultimately fell into the errors of Socinianism.   Towards the close of life, as the story goes, he was one day travelling in a coach, when a lady who sat beside him entered into religious conversation. Having recently read the hymn in question, she enquired of him what he thought about it. Robinson endeavoured to avoid the enquiry, and sought to turn the conversation in another direction. But the lady continued to express her admiration of the hymn, and the great comfort which it had afforded her.   He heard her with deep emotion, and bursting into tears, said, "Madam, I am the poor unhappy author who composed that hymn many years ago, and I would give a thousand worlds, if I had them, to enjoy the feelings I then experienced."

Having thrown out the foregoing brief outline of the rise and progress of psalmody and hymnology in this country, we shall be better prepared to enter upon an examination of our own invaluable Hymn Book.

Amongst the hymn writers just mentioned, the four Wesleys, father and three sons, especially the brother Charles, have acquired deserved

c

and universal fame; and although Montgomery and others have placed Dr. Watts at the head of the list, many think that Charles Wesley is equally entitled to the palm, in which opinion we heartily join.

The obligations under which the Methodist people are laid to these great and good men can never be adequately told. In their active labours, especially those of John Wesley, immense and enduring good was wrought, in the conversion of tens of thousands of immortal souls, and in the establishment of a great evangelistic system which is destined to take a prominent part in the subjugation of the world to Christ. In this undertaking, especially in the early part of it, he was greatly assisted by his brother Charles. The tomb of Sir Christopher Wren, in St. Paul's, London, of which edifice he was the architect, bears the following inscription,—" If you wish to see his monument, look around." And so if we want to see the memorials of the Wesleys we must look around us in the cities, towns, and villages of this kingdom, and in every quarter of the globe. We may behold the effects of their arduous toil and faithful labours in the thousands of beautiful and noble sanctuaries, in the large and flourishing societies, in the net work of connexional arrangements, and in the mighty and multitudinous agencies which Methodism has put in operation. Not only in their active labours have they left behind them untold blessings, but in their literary productions they have conferred an immense boon upon the world. This may be discovered by looking over the long list of works which John Wesley published, as well as the numerous poetic effusions of his brother Charles, estimated to be about six thousand six hundred. Of each of these good men it may be said, " He being dead, yet speaketh." John Wesley in his prose, and Charles Wesley in his poetry, are speaking in almost every language under heaven. Through the instrumentality of the Wesleyan Missionaries, the hymns of Charles have been translated into many languages, and they are greatly accelerating the arrival of that period which Dr. Watts anticipates in his well known lines, when

> People and realms of every tongue,
> Dwell on His love with sweetest song.

It is, however, to the Hymn Book now in use amongst us that we wish to call the reader's attention. It cannot fail to interest a lover of that volume to know how such a collection of precious hymns was brought together. Many of those which form the present book were published originally in small detatched portions at different periods of time. The first volume was issued in 1738, and bore the following title: "A Collection of Psalms and Hymns, London. Printed in the year MDCCXXXVIII." This was a compilation by John Wesley, and has no name either of author or printer. It includes hymns from Watts, Kenn, Norris, Herbert, and others; but none by the Wesleys, excepting a few of John's translations. In 1739, another volume was published, called, "Hymns and Sacred Poems, by John and Charles Wesley. Printed by W. Strahan, and sold by James Hutton, bookseller, at the Bible and Sun, without Temple bar; and at Mr. Bray's, a brazier, in Little Britain." Others followed at various periods, some containing between two and three hundred hymns, and others only twelve, twenty, or thirty. These were issued under various titles, such as, "Hymns for the Watch Night";

"Hymns for the Nativity of our Lord";
"Hymns for Times of Trouble and Persecution"; "Hymns for those that seek, and those
that have, Redemption in the Blood of Christ";
"Hymns on the Trinity"; "Funeral Hymns";
"Hymns on the Lord's Supper"; and many
others. Forty one of these productions, including other effusions of the two Wesleys, were
published between the years 1738 and 1777.
Amongst these was the celebrated Shilling
Hymn Book, consisting of 132 pages, and
called "Hymns and Spiritual Songs, for the
use of Real Christians of all Denominations."
This book was a marvel of cheapness above a
hundred years ago, and its popularity was
proved by the fact that in little more than
twenty years twenty-one editions were called
for, and published.

In the year 1779, a selection was made by
John Wesley from all the preceding works,
which, with the addition of other hymns, was
formed into one volume, and usually called
"THE LARGE HYMN BOOK." The cover of the
Methodist Magazine for October 1779, contains the following announcement :—"Proposals
for Printing, (by Subscription), A Collection

of Hymns, for the use of the People called
Methodists, intended to be used in all their
Congregations. Conditions,—I. This Collection will contain about five hundred hymns,
and upwards of four hundred pages. II. It is
now nearly ready for the press, and will be
printed with all expedition. III. The price
is *three shillings* : half to be paid at the time of
subscribing, the other half at the delivery of the
book, *sewed*. IV. Booksellers *only*, subscribing
for six copies, shall have a seventh gratis." The
price of this book was three shillings sewed,
and four shillings bound. Mr. Wesley bestowed
the utmost care upon it. His correspondence
with the preachers, as well as his remarks in
the preface to the volume, evidence the great
concern he felt respecting it. It was one of his
greatest and best achievements, he felt the im-
portance of the undertaking, and we need not
be surprised that he should be anxious about
its success. In writing to one of the superintendents, he says, "One thing more I desire,
that you would read the proposals for the
general Hymn Book in every society, and
procure as many subscribers as you can. By
your diligence and exactness in these particulars

I shall judge whether you are qualified to act as
an Assistant or not. Pray send me word in
January how many subscriptions you have pro-
cured in your circuit."

This undertaking proved a complete success,
a second edition was required the year following, and a third the year after that, while in
fifteen years no less than nine editions were
called for. This collection was substantially the
same as the one now in use, with the exception
of what is called the Supplement, which was
not published until fifty years afterwards. We
say *substantially* the same, for there were some
hymns of an inferior character omitted in sub-
sequent editions, and others of a superior order
inserted ; the number of such alterations was
not large, amounting to between twenty and
thirty on the whole.

We have said that this Large Hymn Book
was published under the special and careful
supervision of John Wesley. If many of the
hymns were seen in their original form, and
compared with their improved state as they
appear in the present volume, it would be at
once perceived how skilfully and diligently he
used his pruning hand. This remark applies

to the productions of his brother Charles, as well as to other authors. Montgomery observes with considerable truthfulness, " The severer taste of John greatly tempered the extravagance of Charles, pruned his luxuriances, and restrained his impetuosity." The strong and eulogistic terms employed in the preface to the Hymn Book, and the severe remarks about altering the hymns, may seem strange, coming from one who took such liberties with other men's productions; yet in this, as in many other things, a hundred years experience has proved the correctness of his opinions. What he said in 1779, the date of the preface, might be repeated in 1868, " I am persuaded no such hymn book as this has been printed in the English language."

Immediately after Mr. Wesley's death this noble work was greatly tampered with, alterations were made, and hymns inserted of a very inferior sort. This became a considerable grievance, and in 1799, the Conference took up the matter and appointed a committee to examine into and correct the abuse. The following resolution was inserted in the Minutes; " That Dr. Coke, Brother Storey, Brother Moore, and

Brother Clark, be appointed to reduce the large hymn book to its primitive simplicity, as published in the second edition, with liberty to add a word now and then by way of note, to explain a difficult passage for the sake of the unlearned, and a discretionary power is given in respect to the additional hymns." In several of the older editions may be seen those notes of explanation, " now and then" to be inserted. The advanced intelligence of the people having rendered them unnecessary, they have disappeared from all modern editions. The result of the above named committee's deliberations was the issuing of an improved edition in 1803, which made the fifteenth in succession. In 1808, the twentieth was printed, in which also a few alterations were made.

For some years the Connexion continued to use this volume, until it was felt that so large and increasing a body of people required a greater variety of hymns, and more adapted to the mixed congregations worshipping in the sanctuaries of Methodism, and especially for festival occasions. This want was met to some extent by the addition of the SUPPLEMENT, which was published in 1831, by which means

D

209 more hymns were supplied, bringing the
total up to 770. These 770 hymns comprise
nearly 4000 verses, some of four, some of six,
and some of eight lines in a verse, and composed in upwards of twenty different metres.

The total number given in the hymn book
is 769, but owing to some mistake there are
two which bear the heading 45, which will make
the whole what has just been named.

The execution of this work was committed
to the hands of the Rev. R. Watson, the Rev.
T. Jackson, and Dr. Bunting. In sending it
forth they say in the advertisement,—" The
following Supplement is designed to furnish a
greater number of hymns suitable for public
worship, for festivals, and for occasional services, than are found in that invaluable collection
in common use, which the piety and genius of
the Wesleys bequeathed to the societies raised
up by their ministry."

One great object gained by the publication of
the Supplement was, not only a large addition
of valuable hymns, but the securing of a copyright to the Connexion. It had long been found
that cheap and very inferior editions of the
Large Hymn Book had been issued by private

booksellers, to the great pecuniary disadvantage of the Book Room. Steps were therefore taken to obtain a copyright by purchasing from the heirs of Charles Wesley his literary remains, from which some of his best unpublished hymns were selected, which, along with others, were published by the Conference. The compilers say in their preface, " As several of the hymns in this collection are selected from the papers of Mr. Charles Wesley above referred to, and have not before been published, a copyright is established in this Supplement; and all pirated editions are rendered liable to legal process." By these means an effectual check was put to what had grown into a great abuse, and a complete, uniform, and authentic copy of the Hymn Book was thus for the first time prepared for the congregations of Methodism in all parts of the world. This copyright arrangement only included the Supplement, which at first was published in a separate form, but subsequently being bound up with the Large Hymn Book, a complete Collection could only be obtained by possessing both in one, so that the law now practically affects them both.

Not the least valuable part of the volume is

its clear and useful INDEX, by means of which instant reference can be made to every hymn, and every verse, the whole being placed in alphabetical order, with the subjects arranged, as well as the passages of Scripture more particularly illustrated by certain portions of the hymns, some of which supply the best experimental comments and expositions of God's holy word that can possibly be found. The labour in preparing this Index must have been very considerable, but its convenience to both ministers and people has proved proportionately great.

It would doubtless be a great improvement, and very much simplify the giving out of the hymns, if the paging were to be discontinued, and only the number of the hymn retained. By giving out both at the same time confusion often ensues, more especially to persons not familiar with our hymn book. It is a matter of opinion whether the giving out of an entire verse at once, or only a portion of it, is the best. The law of the Connexion unquestionably declares that the latter shall be the practice, which law many true-hearted Methodists think is "more honoured in the breach than the observance." Others, however, are inclined to the

old two line custom, not merely because it is
the old way, but they think that, notwithstanding some few literary incongruities, and musical
inconveniences, it best serves the purposes of
edification and devotion.

Such were the circumstances which placed in
the hands of "the people called Methodists" a
book so greatly beloved and so universally
admired.   Doggerel rhymes and trashy hymns
are now completely banished from our congregations.   In the early days of Methodism the
old preachers occasionally favoured their hearers
with hymns of their own composing.   William
Darney, a Scotchman, or, as he was often called
"Scotch Willie," published in 1751 a volume
entitled, " A Collection of Hymns," (pp. 196,
12mo.) the first of which included 104 verses,
common metre, and consisted of descriptions of
the work of God in the various towns and villages where he laboured.   He says in the preface
that his habit was " to sing some verses at the
beginning of the hymn, then to read over the
rest until he came near the end, when he sung
a verse or two at the close, which had the ten-
dency to open the understandings of the people,
and make them more attentive to the sermon."

Scotch Willie was a zealous and noted preacher in his day ; he entered the ministry in 1742, and died in 1799. His poetic gifts were not of a high order, and, like many others, he fell into the temptation of printing his effusions. These unauthorised productions were always looked upon by Mr. Wesley with disapprobation. At a later period when some of the preachers sought to introduce into the public service hymns of their own making, he strongly set his face against it, as the following letter to one of the Superintendents will show. " You did exactly right in not countenancing hymns not publicly received among us. Were we to encourage little poets we should soon be over-run. But there is not the least pretence for using any new hymns at Christmas, as my brother's Christmas hymns are some of the finest compositions in the English language." We may smile as we picture to ourselves the brawny Scotchman giving out and singing with a loud shrill voice his own doggerel effusions, but we ought to feel grateful to our honoured founder for his firmness in preventing such irregularities, and for preserving the purity and dignity of public worship amongst us.

Whilst Mr. Wesley displayed so much care in providing the connexion with suitable hymns, he was equally concerned that proper and appropriate tunes should be used in singing them. He speaks in the strongest terms against the old village choirs, with the drawling of the parish clerk, and the hum-drum droning of the village congregation. We find him in his correspondence with the preachers often calling their attention to this subject, such as, " Preach frequently on singing,"—" Exhort every one in the congregation to sing,"—" In every large society let them learn to sing." As early as 1746 we find the following question asked in the Conference, " How shall we guard more effectually against formality in singing ?" In addition to other answers, we read,—" 4, By suiting the tunes to the hymns. 5, By often stopping short and asking the people, ' Now, do you know what you said last ? Did it suit your case ? Did you sing it as to God ?'" In the Conference of 1765, the question is asked, " What can be done to make the people sing better ? Answer. 1, Teach them to sing by note, and to sing our tunes first ; 2, Take care they do not sing too slow ; 3, Exhort all that

can in every congregation to sing ; 4, Set them
right that sing wrong. Be patient." See also
the Minutes for 1768. To assist in promoting
good singing in the congregations he published
several works on the subject. As early as 1742
a volume was issued entitled " A Collection of
Tunes set to Music as they are sung at the
Foundery." Also, " Sacred Melody," " The
Grounds of Music," and " Sacred Harmony."
The work entitled " Sacred Melody, or a choice
Collection of Psalm and Hymn Tunes," contains full instructions how to learn the notes,
and how to exercise the voice. It includes a
hundred and fourteen tunes, some of which
possess good and solid music, but others would
no doubt produce a smile amongst modern
choirs. A preface is inserted, as well as a hundred and forty nine selected hymns, for which
the tunes are adapted. The Introduction to
the musical part of the work is thoroughly like
John Wesley. It is as follows, " That this part
of Divine worship may be the more acceptable
to God, as well as the more profitable to
yourself and others, be careful to observe the
following Directions,—1, Learn *these* Tunes
before you learn any others ; afterwards learn

as many as you please. 2, Sing them exactly as they are printed here, without altering or mending them at all; and if you have learned to sing them otherwise, unlearn it as soon as you can. 3, Sing *All*. See that you join with the congregation as frequently as you can. Let not a slight degree of weakness or weariness hinder you. If it is a cross to you, take it up and you will find a blessing. 4, Sing *lustily*, and with a good courage. Beware of singing as if you were half dead, or half asleep; but lift up your voice with strength. Be no more afraid of your voice now, nor more ashamed of its being heard, than when you sung the songs of Satan. 5, Sing · *modestly*. Do not bawl so as to be heard above, or distinct from the rest of the congregation, that you may not destroy the harmony; but strive to unite your voices together so as to make one clear melodious sound. 6, Sing *in Time*; whatever time is sung be sure to keep with it. Do not run before, nor stay behind it; but attend close to the leading voices, and move therewith as exactly as you can; and take care that you sing not *too slow*. This drawling way naturally steals on all who are lazy, and it is high time to drive

E

it out from amongst us, and sing all our Tunes just as quick as we did at first. 7, Above all sing *spiritually*. Have an eye to God in every word you sing. Aim at pleasing Him more than yourself, or any other creature : In order to this attend strictly to the sense of what you sing, and see that your heart is not carried away with the sound, but offered to God continually, so shall your singing be such as the Lord will approve of here, and reward when he cometh in the clouds of heaven." After giving a carefully prepared Table of the Grounds of Sacred Melody, he says, " Let each of these Lessons be got off perfectly, and by heart, in the order they are here placed, so that they all may be sung readily, and exactly, both in Tune and Time."

We trace the devout and superior character of our congregational singing to these early and careful efforts of Mr. Wesley, and we hesitate not to say, without the least sectarian pride, that amongst no christian people is the service of song in the temple of the Lord conducted with greater reverence, earnestness, and decorum than by the Wesleyan Methodists.

Having said thus much respecting the rise

and formation of the Hymn Book now in use, we will next proceed to notice the authorship of the various hymns. The critical examinations of the last twenty years have thrown much light upon this branch of our subject, so that the writer of nearly every hymn can now be pretty accurately ascertained. The following summary has been taken from "Kirk's Original Titles of the Wesleyan Hymns," a useful little work, and generally considered to be correct.

Addison Joseph	3	Olivers, Rev. Thomas .	3
Bakewell, John	1	Rhodes, Rev. Benj. ...	2
Brackenbury, R. C.	1	Steele, Miss	3
Bulmer, Mrs.	1	Stennett, Rev. Joseph	1
Bunting, Rev. W. M. ...	1	Tate and Brady,	2
Cowper, William	2	Toplady, Rev. A.	1
Doddridge, Rev. Dr. ...	10	Unknown,	1
Dryden, John	1	Watts, Rev. Dr.	66
Hart, Rev. Joseph	1	Wesley, Rev. Charles .	626
Ken, Bishop	2	Wesley, Rev. John ...	*33
Merrick, Rev. James ...	1	Wesley, Rev. Saml. jun.	6
More, Rev. Dr. Henry .	2	Wesley, Rev. Saml. sen.	1

This enumeration shows that upwards of *six hundred and twenty hymns are from the pen of Charles Wesley alone.* With this striking fact before us we see how justly entitled he is to be

* Including his translations.

called the Poet of Methodism. Great indeed
are the obligations of the churches to this sweet
singer in Israel, whose inspiring strains have
led many a penitent sinner to the Saviour, by
means of which many a hard duty has been
cheerfully performed, and many a heavy cross
has been patiently borne, and in the strength
and gladness which they inspired tens of thousands have triumphed over death, and gone
home to heaven. Well might the good old
Methodist female say, when she heard of his
decease, " Who will poetry for us now ?" Who
does not feel it to be an honour to be connected,
however remotely, with such a man, and such a
name ? As a people we do right to glorify
God in him, and to be thankful to the great
Head of the Church for raising up and giving
us so great a blessing.

We will now endeavour to place before the
reader the names of the different authors, with
a short biographical sketch of each as they
alphabetically rise.

ADDISON.

Hymn 567.   The spacious firmament on high.
,,   592.   When all Thy mercies, O my God.
,,   765.   How are Thy servants blest, O Lord.

Joseph Addison was a distinguished writer and politician, who died in 1719. He was once a Secretary of State under the British Government, and chief contributor to the Spectator, a popular periodical of that day. His life was chequered by severe trials of a domestic nature; his private character was not free from personal indiscretions, but he died trusting in the merits of the great Redeemer.

BAKEWELL.

Hymn 633. Hail Thou once despised Jesus.

John Bakewell was one of the first race of Methodist local preachers, in which capacity he laboured seventy years, and died in 1819, at the advanced age of ninety-eight. Toplady has been named by some, and Charles Wesley by others as the author of this beautiful hymn, but recent evidence has settled the controversy in favour of Bakewell.*

BRACKENBURY, R. C.

Hymn 653. Come, Holy Spirit, raise our songs.

The first three verses of this hymn on the

---

* See an interesting Sketch of Bakewell, by Mr. Stelfox, of Belfast.

Pentecost are the productions of this writer,
and the remainder by Charles Wesley. Mr.
Brackenbury was a gentleman of independent
means, a magistrate in Lincolnshire, and a man
of considerable attainments. He joined the
Methodist Society, became a zealous and most
successful local preacher, and travelled with
Mr. Wesley over many parts of the kingdom.
He was gifted as a poet, and wrote and published some valuable hymns. He died in 1818,
in the sixty-sixth year of his age.

BRADY AND TATE.

Hymn 571.   With glory clad, with strength arrayed,
  „   584.   O render thanks to God above.

Doctor Brady, Chaplain in ordinary, and
Nahum Tate, Poet Laureate to Queen Anne,
were the authors of the New Metrical Version
of the Book of Psalms now in use in the Church
of England, and generally found affixed to the
Prayer Book. The " New Version," as it is
commonly called, was first published in the
reign of William the Third, and superseded the
" Old Version" by Sternhold and Hopkins.
The former is considered more refined, but the
latter more correct. Dr. Adam Clarke said, " I

can sing almost every Psalm in the version by Sternhold and Hopkins as the Psalms of David, I can sing those of the new version as the Psalms of Dr. Brady and Nahum Tate." The two hymns in our Book are amongst the very best of the New Version.

BULMER.

Hymn 737. Thou who hast in Zion laid.

Mrs. Agnes Bulmer was a Wesleyan, and author of a work entitled, "Messiah's Kingdom, and other Poems." She died in 1836. This hymn was written specially to be sung on the occasion of laying the foundation - stone of Oxford Road Wesleyan Chapel, Manchester, and has been used on thousands of similar occasions since that time. It is a valuable and appropriate hymn, but being almost the only one in the book for such services, the need of a few others of different metres is greatly felt by the Connexion.

BUNTING.

Hymn 748. O, God, how often hath Thine ear.

The Rev. W. M. Bunting was the eldest son of the late Dr. Bunting. He was an eloquent preacher, and a poet of no mean order. He contributed largely to the literature of Methodism, and other publications, and, until very recently, was the only living author connected with the Wesleyan Hymn Book. He died November 9th, 1866, in the sixty-first year of his age.

COWPER.

Hymn 559. God moves in a mysterious way.
   „ 663. O for a closer walk with God.

William Cowper was the well-known Christian poet whose works have obtained a world wide fame. He was the author of many of the Olney Hymns, amongst which is the familiar one commencing,—" There is a fountain filled with blood." The life of Cowper was full of melancholy interest. He was subject to fits of awful depression, and yet, strange to say, it was on recovering from one of those fits that he wrote that most amusing and laughter stirring old favourite John Gilpin. A circumstance is recorded in connection with the 559 hymn which invests it with painful interest. In 1773, when in one of those seasons of dismal gloom, he was led to believe it was the will of God that he should drown himself in a particular part of the river Ouse. He ordered his coachman to drive him to the place, and the man obeyed, not knowing his master's intentions. But notwithstanding he was well acquainted with the neighbourhood, he could not find the particular spot referred to. After driving about several hours the man was obliged to admit that he had lost his road. On reaching home poor Cowper was so affected by the circumstance that he sat down and composed that beautiful and well known hymn beginning, " God moves in a mysterious way," etc., under the title of Light shining in Darkness.

DRYDEN.

Hymn 654. Creator, Spirit, by whose aid.

John Dryden was a celebrated poet, and such was the fame which he acquired that he had the distinguished honour at his death of being interred in Westminster Abbey. Some have asserted that the hymns 564, 565, and 566, were written by him, but we know not on what authority this supposition rests. There is strong evidence that they are all three Charles Wesley's. The one ascribed to Dryden is a

F

translation from the ancient Latin hymn, Veni Creator Spiritus.

DODDRIDGE.

Doctor Philip Doddridge was born in 1702, and died in 1751. He was the Pastor of a dissenting Church at Northampton, and the author of several valuable works on divinity, including the Family Expositor, and the well known Rise and Progress of Religion in the Soul. The amount of good effected by the latter has been immense. " It is an interesting fact," says Josiah Conder, "that the plan of that most popular practical treatise, The Rise and Progress of Religion in the Soul, had been drawn out by Dr. Watts, but, compelled by his growing infirmities to abandon his purpose, he relinquished the task to Dr. Doddridge, who, after some hesitation, yielded to his importunity, and completed the performance." He also wrote some sweet and beautiful hymns, which for gentleness and purity very much resemble the spirit of their author. Ten of his are inserted in the Wesleyan Hymn Book, as already stated.

HART.

Hymn 588. This, this is the God we adore.

The Rev. Joseph Hart was a dissenting Minister and Pastor of Jewin-Street Chapel, Poplar, London. He wrote a considerable number of hymns, a collection of which he published in 1759. They are thoroughly calvinistic and quaint, but, in general, pious and devout. He died in 1768, and so greatly was he respected that 20,000 people, it is said, attended his funeral. His name deserves respect on account of the old and favorite hymn—"This, this is the God we adore," etc. It is the closing part of a long one commencing "No prophet or dreamer of dreams."

KEN.

Hymn 757. Awake my soul, and with the sun.
  ,, 758. Glory to Thee, my God, this night.

Thomas Ken, Bishop, died in 1710. He was called to pass through a changeful and adventurous life. He was raised to the See of Bath and Wells, and was one of the seven bishops who were imprisoned for resisting the tyranny of James the 2nd. He was the author of the well known Morning and Evening hymns, hymns which are associated with our earliest and happiest recollections. Montgomery says, " Bishop Ken has laid the church of Christ under obligations by his three hymns, Morning, Evening, and Midnight. Had he endowed three hospitals, he might have been less a benefactor to posterity." The grand old Doxology, " Praise God from whom all blessings flow," is a perpetual honour to his name. An interesting circumstance it is said, once occurred in connection with one of these hymns. An excursion train from the country filled with operatives was on its way to the Great Exhibition, in 1851. In one of the carriages was a vulgar individual, whose tongue was employed in making obscene remarks. He was rebuked by an indignant female, but finding that she could produce no impression upon him, she struck up, " Glory to Thee, my God, this night." Others joined their voices; the occupants of the next carriage caught the tune, and the tongue of the vile fellow was put to silence by the voices of united praise.

MERRICK.

Hymn 585.   Far as Creation's bounds extend.

The Rev. James Merrick was a clergyman of the Church of England. This hymn is taken from his work on the Psalms. The lines, " In every sorrow of the heart," etc., are not his.

MORE.

Hymn 456.   Father, if still we justly claim.
  „   457.   On all the earth Thy Spirit shower.

Doctor Henry More, another clergyman of the Church of England, was born at Grantham in 1614, and died in 1687. He was a man of considerable genius, and an undoubted scholar. He bore an excellent character, but was somewhat peculiar in his views. He was a great admirer of Plato, and believed him to have been divinely inspired. Under this impression he wrote a work called Psycho Zoia, a Song of the Soul, in which he teaches a sort of platonized christianity. He was also a writer of

hymns. The two above were amongst his best,
but they were much improved, and in a great
measure re-written by Mr. Wesley before he
admitted them into his collection.

OLIVERS.

Hymn 669.   The God of Abraham praise.
   „   670.   Though nature's strength decays.
   „   671.   Before the great Three-One.

The Rev. Thomas Olivers was one of the
early Methodist preachers. He was a native
of North Wales, and before his conversion was
a wild and drunken profligate, by trade a shoe-
maker.   After his conversion he became a
powerful and laborious preacher, and for many
years was employed by Mr. Wesley as corrector
of his press, and for some time was editor of
the Magazine.   He died in 1799, and was
buried in the Wesley vault, City-Road, London.
John Fletcher said of him, " His talents as a
writer, as a logician, a poet, and a composer of
sacred music are known to those who have
looked into his compositions." As a controver-
sialist he possessed considerable tact and force,
especially on the doctrine of Calvinism, which
often brought him into collision with men of

that school. He was a brave soldier in that hot campaign when the Wesleys, Hill, and Toplady fought, and struck such heavy blows. Southey called him " the fiery minded Welshman." It was of Olivers in his literary occupation that Toplady used his bitter sarcasms. He makes Mr. Wesley say,

> " I've Tommy Olivers the cobbler,
> No stall in England holds a nobler ;
> A wight of talent universal,
> Whereof I'll give a brief rehearsal,
> He with one brandish of his quill,
> Can knock down Toplady and Hill."

As a poet he had superior gifts. Montgomery said " That noble ode, ' The God of Abraham praise,' though the essay of an unlettered man, claims special honour. There is not in our language a lyric of more majestic style, more elevated thought, or more glorious imagery." Blackwood's Magazine, in one of its critiques, says, " This hymn is one of the noblest odes in the English language." Stevens in his stirring History of Methodism, says, " There are stanzas in this ode fit for archangels to sing." To such an extent did the public appreciate its worth, that in 1799, the year of his death, it had reached its *thirtieth* edition. The grand and simple tune called *Leoni* to which these words are generally sung, is a Hebrew Melody, which was used at the time in the Jewish Synagogue. Olivers and John Bakewell happened to be present at one of the services and heard the music, with which the former was greatly delighted. Being acquainted with the Priest, whose name was Leoni, Olivers requested him to adapt it to his words, which he did, and afterwards called it by his name. The tune itself is a very ancient one, and is supposed by some to have been sung by the Saviour and his disciples when they celebrated the first sacramental feast. He wrote also an impressive and majestic hymn on the Last Judgment, consisting of thirty six verses. Hymn the 66th, " Lo he comes," etc., has long been ascribed to Olivers, but satisfactory evidence has recently been adduced to the contrary. It is now generally admitted that Charles Wesley wrote it, and in all respects it is worthy of his name.*

* See letters for and against in the Wesleyan Magazine for 1861, pages 63 and 244, also in the Methodist Recorder for April 24th, 1868, and Lyra Britannica.

RHODES.

Hymn 637. My heart and voice I raise.
 „   638. Jerusalem divine.

The Rev. Benjamin Rhodes was a Wesleyan Minister who commenced his ministry in 1766, and died in 1816. He acquired a position of influence and respectability in the connexion, and was a frequent correspondent of Mr. Wesley. Mr. T. P. Bunting in his life of Dr. Bunting, says, when speaking of Mr. Rhodes, " I see in the face of Rhodes, as his portrait appears in the second volume of the Arminian Magazine, characteristics which his own modest record of his life does not suggest, but which I should expect to find in the author of the hymns on the kingdom of Christ in the Supplement to Wesley's Collection. In the heart, as in the brow of the writer of those stanzas, there must have dwelt a solemn and lofty piety, an earnest evangelism, and a patient longing for the coming of the triumphant Saviour."*

* "I remember," said an old man, the other day, his face brightening with the recollection which he was calling up, " I remember some years ago a minister coming into our neighbourhood to preach. He was a good man, and a good preacher, but I can mind his singing much better than his sermons. He used to preach not far from where

STENNETT.

Hymn 583.   Again our weekly labours end.

The Rev. Joseph Stennett was a Baptist Minister, who died in 1713.

STEELE.

Hymn 580.   Great God this hallowed day of Thine.
,,   722.   Almighty Maker of my frame.
,,   746.   Father of mercies in Thy word.

Miss Anne Steele was the daughter of a Baptist minister.   She wrote some touching and valuable hymns, from which these three were selected.   She finished her course in 1778.

I lived, and when I saw the people flocking to the chapel, I used to go to hear the famous singer.   Ah, he was a singer!   And I believe one great secret of his singing was that his heart was in it.   His voice was like an angel's, as they say, though I never heard an angel sing; but I can scarcely think that an angel, or any other singer could beat that happy looking preacher.   He was a man with a long face, and a high bald head.   And his eyes used to sparkle as he sang, as if the hymns were coming up from his soul, and so they did.   There was one hymn I always liked to hear him sing, he would sing it after the sermon; it was one of his own composing, and the tune was his too, I learnt to sing it myself, and I taught my boy to sing it; and sometimes, long after that singing preacher was gone to his own "Jerusalem divine," my boy and I, and three or four more, used to get together of an evening. and sing it in full harmony.   Oh, it was so rich; and it seemed to lift one toward heaven while we sang."   See *Christopher's Hymn Writers* on the Rev. B. Rhodes.

TOPLADY.

Hymn 624.   Rock of Ages, cleft for me.

The Rev. Augustus Toplady was a Devon-shire clergyman, who died in 1775. He rendered himself notorious by his strong cal-vinistic opinions, and his bitter opposition to the Wesleys. So intense and ultra were his views on calvinism that when dying he demanded to be carried to the house of God, and there uttered his last public avowal of his principles. He wrote a harsh and discreditable book against John Wesley bearing the follow-ing expressive title, "The Old Fox Tarred and Feathered." This was Toplady's shady side, he had, nevertheless, a bright one as well, for, with these exceptions, he was a zealous and faithful minister of the gospel. He wrote some useful hymns, several of which, along with some by other authors, were published in 1776, the year after his decease, one of which has immor-talized his name, viz., Rock of Ages, cleft for me. A few have questioned his claim to it. Richard Watson ascribed it to Charles Wesley. See his letters in the Magazine for 1832, and the Methodist Recorder for June 19, 1868. The evidence in favour of Toplady is not now disputed. It has been thought however that he derived his inspiration from a hymn on the Lord's Supper published in one of the early collections by the Wesleys, beginning—

Rock of Israel, cleft for me.

In the form in which it appears in our book it has undergone several great improvements. Its original title was "A Living and Dying Prayer for the Holiest Believer in the world." The late Prince Albert repeated portions of it in his affliction, and derived great consolation from it when dying. Dr. Pomeroy of America, says, that when he was in Constantinople he visited an Armenian Church, and was greatly pleased with the singing which he heard there. The worshippers, he says, sang with their eyes closed, while tears ran down their cheeks, under deep emotion. He asked what hymn they were singing which so affected them, and was pleased to hear that it was "Rock of Ages," etc. Thousands of departing saints have breathed out their souls in its exalted strains, and as they sank into the arms of death have uttered with their quivering breath, Rock of Ages, etc.

WATTS.

Hymn 730. Give me the wings of faith to rise.

„ 738. How pleasant, how divinely fair.

„ 741. How large the promise, how divine.

„ 751. The promise of my Father's love.

„ 769. I give immortal praise.

Doctor Isaac Watts was born at Southampton in 1674. and died in 1748. He was the pastor of a dissenting congregation in London, and the author of some valuable works on divinity, logic, history, metrical psalms, hymns, and lyric poems. He wrote some of the noblest hymns in the English language, and many also that were extremely feeble. There are few writers of hymns in whose productions are combined more of the extremes of strength and feebleness, of sublimity and puerility, than in those of Doctor Watts.* His very best may be found in the Wesleyan Hymn Book. Many of them have undergone great improvements at the hands of John Wesley.†

* The Rev. Richard Watson says, " Many of Dr. Watts' compositions begin well, often nobly, and then fall off into dulness and puerility, and not a few are utterly worthless; as being poor in thought, and still more so in expression."

† " John Wesley's touches are, for the most part, delicate and effective. By the slightest stroke he sometimes turns weakness into

Many interesting facts might be given illustrative of Dr. Watts' hymns, but want of room prevents us doing so. We give however two or three.

Hymn 224, I'll praise my Maker while I've breath.

This beautiful song of praise is a great favourite with many. Almost the last articulate sentence which fell from the lips of John Wesley was a part of the first line of this hymn. In his departing moments he tried to repeat the whole line, but failed to do so. As the breath was leaving his body he gasped,—" I'll praise—I'll praise,—Farewell," and all was over. A remarkable circumstance is mentioned in the life of Dr. Bunting in connection with this hymn. Soon after the Doctor's conversion, he, along with some others, conducted prayer meetings in different parts of Manchester. One was held in Cross-Lane, at the house of one James Ashcroft, a mechanic. Twenty years afterwards, the same man, with his son and brother, and

strength, common places into beauties, and irregularity into order. A transforming word or two from him makes questionable things pure, and calls up grandeur from what is puerile and mean."

Christopher's Hymn Writers.

one William Holden, were all convicted of mur-
dering two women at Pendleton. While standing upon the scaffold with their faces covered
ready to be launched into eternity, there arose
a dull and muffled sound which proceeded from
the lips of these wretched men. Each joined
in singing this hymn until they came to the last
line, " While life, and thought, and being last,"
but just as they reached the words, "While life
and thought—" the drop fell, and their voices
were hushed in the silence of death.

Hymn 316. Eternal Power, whose high abode.

This hymn is painfully associated with the
death of the eloquent Dr. Beaumont. On Sunday, January 21st, 1855, he entered Waltham
Street Chapel, Hull, to conduct the morning
worship, and selected this hymn for opening the
service. He gave out the two first lines of the
second verse with great solemnity and power,
and while the congregation was singing the
next two lines,

" And ranks of shining ones around," etc.

he sank down in the pulpit, and his fine, noble
spirit took its instant flight to heaven. He

died in full harness, and fell on one of the high places of the field.

We come now to notice the hymns of the Wesleys. As previously stated, the Hymn Book contains contributions from all four, viz., the father and three sons. We will point out the authorship of all but those by Charles, and then proceed to give some facts and incidents in connection with many of his.

S. WESLEY, SEN.

Hymn 22. Behold the Saviour of mankind.

The Rev. Samuel Wesley was Rector of Epworth, and father of Messrs. John, Charles, and Samuel Wesley. He was born 1662, and died in 1735. When the Parsonage house at Epworth was burnt down in 1709, three or four sheets of music were picked up amidst the ruins which bore evident marks of the fire. Connected with the notes were the words of this 22nd hymn. The son of Charles Wesley wrote on one of these sheets the following,— "These words were written by my grandfather, the Rev. Samuel Wesley, Sen." The last verse

in the hymn as found in the present book was
not in the original one. It was probably composed by John Wesley to put in the place of
two others, which he thought proper to omit.

S. WESLEY, JUN.

Hymn 46.	The morning flowers display their sweets.
„ 544.	The Lord of Sabbath let us praise.
„ 561.	Hail, Father, whose creating call.
„ 601.	Hail, God the Son, in glory crowned.
„ 613.	From whence these dire portents arise.
„ 649.	Hail, Holy Ghost! Jehovah! third.

The Rev. Samuel Wesley, Jun., was the
eldest son of the Wesley family, and was a
clergyman of the Church of England, but was
for some years at the head of a scholastic establishment at Tiverton, where he died in 1739.
He was the author of some devotional, as well
as satirical and humorous poetry, which was
published in a large quarto volume in 1736.
He kept aloof altogether from his brothers in
their Methodistical proceedings, and was antag-
onistic to the movement.

J. WESLEY.

Hymn 4.	Ho, every one that thirsts, draw nigh.
„ 68.	How happy is the pilgrim's lot.

The Rev. John Wesley was born at Epworth in 1703, in 1724 he was elected a Fellow of Lincoln College, Oxford, where he became Greek Lecturer. In 1735 he went to Georgia as a missionary, and after labouring there some time he returned to England. After experiencing the pardon of his sins, and the renewing grace of God, he commenced his long and extraordinary course of labours which spread over a period of more than half a century, and which resulted in the formation of the Connexion of the People called Methodists. He finished his course March 2nd, 1791, aged 88 years. As his life is so familiar to most of our readers we have not deemed any further record necessary.

Beside the above named original hymns, the volume contains twenty six translations by John Wesley, viz., twenty four from the German, one from the French, and one from the

---

* It is supposed that a few others belong to John, which have been ascribed to Charles, but the particular hymns cannot with certainty be determined.

Spanish. It is but right to say that much of
the spirit and beauty of these translations is
due to the translator, who clothed the originals
with language, and invested them with a power
which has placed them amongst the most
majestic and devout productions. We have
also given the names of the authors, as far as
they could possibly be ascertained. Great
care has been taken to be correct on this point,
inasmuch as many mistakes have been committed in ascribing these beautiful effusions to their
original writers.*

PAUL GERHARDT.

Hymn 23.	Extended on a cursed tree.
„ 373.	Jesu, Thy boundless love to me.
„(?)610.	O God of Gods, in whom combine.
„ †673.	Commit thou all thy griefs.
„ 674.	Give to the winds thy fears.

PARTLY BY COUNT ZINZENDORF, AND JOHN AND ANNA NITSCHMAN.

Hymn 26.   I thirst Thou wounded Lamb of God.

---

* The writer gratefully acknowledges the kind assistance of Mr. C.
D. Hardcastle of Keighley, in tracing the authorship of the German
hymns, as well as much valuable help which he has afforded during
the preparation of this work.

† This beautiful hymn was written by Paul Gerhardt under painfully
interesting circumstances. The bitter persecution of the Romanists
obliged him with his young wife to fly from their home, and escape

for their lives. They left the city of Erfurt amidst the rigours of winter, and suffered great hardships from the inclemency of the weather, which was aggravated by the fact of the latter being near her confinement. Weary and exhausted, and almost heart broken, the poor young creature began to bitterly complain, and to ask whether some place of rest and safety could not be found. Whereupon her husband wrote this and the following most touching and encouraging hymns, which formed originally one effusion. Tradition relates a most marvellous circumstance connected with Gerhardt's parents, his birth, and early life, which we regret our space will not allow us to insert.

* The celebrated Richard Cobden, after struggling awhile with the last enemy, fell asleep in Christ with the beautiful words of this hymn upon his lips, "Thee will I love, my strength, my tower."

63

C. P. RITCHTER.

Hymn 338. Thou Lamb of God, thou Prince of peace.

The writer cannot pass away from this hymn without alluding to a circumstance which greatly affected him many years ago. The late Rev. George Morley, then governor of Woodhouse Grove School, was a great sufferer during the latter part of his days. Sometimes his pains were most excruciating. One day the writer saw him in one of his severest paroxisms, when, with tears streaming down his face, and with a sweet patient smile upon his countenance, he grasped the hand of the enquirer after his health and repeated the third verse of this hymn, beginning " When pain o'er my weak flesh prevails."

The Rev. John Hessel, a Wesleyan Minister, a fine young man who died in the prime of life, just before he finished his course, one day said, after a season of great prostration and suffering, " Within the last few days I have very much enjoyed the hymns headed, " For Believers Suffering," and more especially one of them. He then turned to the 338th hymn, beginning, " Thou Lamb of God," etc., and pointing to the third verse, " When pain o'er my weak flesh prevails," he said, "That just suits my case, I know not how many times I have repeated it to day."

G. TERSTEEGEN.

„ 339. (?)O Thou, to whose all searching sight.
„ 344. Thou hidden love of God, whose height.
„ 494. Lo! God is here! let us adore.

ANNA DOBER.

„ 350. Holy Lamb, who Thee receive.

FRAYLINGHAUSEN.

„ 353. O Jesus, source of calm repose.

SPANGENBURG.

„ 492. What shall we offer our good Lord.

UNKNOWN. (SPANISH.)

„ 437. O God, my God, my all Thou art.

MADAME BOURIGNON. (FRENCH.)

„ 285. Come Saviour, Jesus, from above.

By some the last has been ascribed to Dr. Byrom, of Manchester, an intimate friend of the Wesleys, and a writer of considerable merit. Mr. Kirk in his Original Titles, gives J. Wesley as the translator.

Hymn 190, by Count Zinzendorf, contained originally a greater number of verses than are found in the Methodist Collection. The two following fine stanzas have been left out,—

This spotless robe the same appears,
When ruined nature sinks in years ;
No age can change its constant hue,
The blood of Christ is ever new.

O, let the dead now hear Thy voice,
Now bid Thy banished ones rejoice ;
Their beauty this, their glorious dress,
Jesus, Thy Blood and Righteousness.

Two of the verses in the present hymn are
not found in some of the early editions. They
bear strong marks of John Wesley's Arminian-
ism, especially the fifth verse,—

Lord, I believe were sinners more,
Than sands upon the ocean shore ;
Thou hast for all a ransom paid,
For all a full atonement made.

At the interment of the Rev. Rowland Hill,
in the chapel where he had so long held forth
the word of life, while the body was being low-
ered into its last resting place, thousands bathed
in tears, and overwhelmed with emotion, sang
the sixth verse,—

When from the dust of death I rise,
To claim my mansion in the skies,
Even then this shall be all my plea,
Jesus hath lived, hath died for me.

I

There is one hymn the authorship of which cannot be ascertained, namely,

560. Lord dismiss us with Thy blessing.

We cannot trace it beyond a "Collection of Hymns, Psalms, and Anthems," by the Rev. E. Smyth, Manchester, in 1793. It appeared in a somewhat altered form in the Wesleyan Hymn Book in 1797. The authorship of another is somewhat doubtful, namely,

647. O Sun of Righteousness arise.

Some give it to Charles, others to John Wesley, and some to Dr. Byrom. Mr. Burgess says, " It is pretty certain that it is not the original composition of either of the brothers, because of the rhyming of the first and third lines being neglected, there not being another such an instance in all their productions."

Having gone over all the hymns and their authors, excepting those of Charles Wesley, we will next proceed to a fuller and more particular consideration of some of those of which he is the known author. We would here suggest a simple and easy plan by which the writer of every hymn may be seen at a glance. Write at the head of every one the author's name, *excepting those by C. Wesley.* This would involve only 143 names, it being understood that all the rest, exclusive of the two unascertained, would belong to him.

Charles Wesley was born at Epworth in 1708, he was an ordained clergyman of the Church of England, accompanied his brother to America, returned in 1736, took an active part in the formation of the Methodist Society, and died in 1788. He left a widow who survived him thirty four years, and died in 1822, aged *ninety six.* His daughter Sarah died in 1828, aged sixty eight ; his son Charles died in 1834, aged seventy seven ; and his youngest son Samuel died in 1837, aged seventy two. Charles and Sarah were never married, but Samuel left several children, one of which is Dr. Wesley, the celebrated organist, who seems to inherit the musical gifts of his distinguished grandfather.

Charles Wesley, Sen., was a genuine christian poet, who in an eminent degree derived his inspiration from above, and climbed the holy summits of mount Zion, as well as the heights of famed Parnassus. The Rev. Thomas Jackson says "He was almost daily exercised in the composition of hymns, his thoughts flowed in numbers; and his deep feelings of joy, and confidence, and zeal could find no adequate expression but in poetry. His sermons appear to have been generally extempore. What he wrote was mostly in sacred verse. His hymns were not the production of a lively imagination gazing upon external objects, nor were they the fruits of hard mental toil. They were the irrepressible effusions of his heart burning with love to God, reposing with absolute and joyous confidénc in the Divine truth and mercy, yearning with affection for the souls of redeemed men, and anticipating the visions of future glory." This is a true description of this celebrated hymnist. The immense number of poetic effusions which he left behind him shews that his very nature was under constant inspiration. In his Journal he mentions an accident of a somewhat serious nature, from which we learn how his thoughts were occupied at the time. He says, " 1743, Monday, May 30th. Near Ripley my horse threw, and fell upon, me. My companion thought I had broke my

neck ; but my leg only was bruised, my hand
sprained, and my head stunned ; which spoiled
my making hymns, or thinking at all till the
next day."

His poetic fire glowed with undiminished
ardour amidst old age, and even unto death.
When bordering upon eighty he frequently
poured forth some beautiful strains with all the
vigour and freshness of youth.   The Rev.
Henry Moore, in his life of Wesley, speaking
of Charles in his old age, says, "He rode every
day, clothed for winter even in summer, a little
horse, grey with age.   When he mounted, if a
subject struck him, he proceeded to expand and
put it in order.   He would write a hymn thus
given him on a card kept for that purpose, with
his pencil, in short hand.   Not unfrequently he
has come to the house in City Road, and having
left the pony in the garden in front, he would
enter crying out, Pen and Ink !   Pen and Ink !
These being supplied, he wrote the hymn he
had been composing.   When this was done, he
would look round on those present, and salute
them with much kindness, ask after their health,
give out a short hymn, and thus put all in mind
of eternity.   He was fond of that stanza upon

these occasions, commencing 'There all the ship's company meet.'"

This holy fire burned upon the altar even when the ravages of death were fast dissolving it. A few days before he died, having been for some time wrapt in silent meditation, he called to Mrs. Wesley and requested her to write, and opening his lips, he dictated the following beautiful lines,—

> In age and feebleness extreme.
> Who shall a sinful worm redeem?
> Jesus, my only hope Thou art,
> Strength of my failing flesh and heart,
> O could I catch a smile from Thee,
> And drop into eternity.

His very tombstone bears the fruit of his own poetic genius. It stands in St. Mary-le-bone church yard, London, and has inscribed upon it the following lines which he composed on the death of one of his dear friends,—

> With poverty of spirit blest,
> Rest happy soul, in Jesus rest.
> A sinner saved, through grace forgiven,
> Redeemed from earth, to reign in heaven.
> Thy labours of unwearied love,
> By Thee forgot, are crowned above,

Crowned through the mercy of thy Lord,
With a free, full, immense reward !*

Such is a brief sketch of this genial, and generous, and warm hearted man. Dr. Stevens, after giving a description of his character and talents, says of him at the close, "He was the best of hymnologists, one of the best preachers, and, with a few pardonable weaknesses, one of the best men of his age. Hundreds of thousands of dying Methodists have blessed his memory, as they have sung or gasped the lyrics in which he has taught them to triumph over death." Before leaving this part of our subject we think it right to state that, beside the many hymns with which our Collection abounds, he wrote some sweet and charming little hymns for young children, amongst which is that universal favourite,—

---

* The record of his death may be found in the Minutes of 1788. It is very brief and simple, and reads as follows:—"Mr. CHARLES WESLEY, who, after spending four score years with much sorrow and pain, quietly retired into Abraham's bosom. He had no disease; but after a gradual decay of some months,

'The weary wheels of life stood still at last.'

His least praise was his talents for poetry, although Dr. Watts did not scruple to say, "that single poem, *Wrestling Jacob*, was worth all the verses he himself had written."

Gentle Jesus, meek and mild,
Look upon a little child ;
Pity my simplicity,
Suffer me to come to Thee.
Fain I would to Thee be brought,
Dearest God forbid it not.
Give to me O Lord a place,
In the kingdom of Thy grace.

Who has not been delighted and affected
whilst listening to those beautiful and simple
words ascending from infant lips to Him who
said, " Suffer little children to come unto Me,"
and who but a man with Charles Wesley's
loving and fatherly heart could have written
such lines ?   Dr. Watts has long had the credit
of its authorship, but this is an entire mistake.
It bears the impress, as it unquestionably is,
the production of the poet of Methodism.

Charles Wesley possessed great sprightly-
ness of wit and genius, and could throw around
adverse and discouraging circumstances sun-
shine and gladness.   Where his preaching failed
his poetry sometimes came to his help.   He
proved the truth of George Herbert's words,—

A verse may find him, who a sermon flies,
And turn delight into a sacrifice.

An instance of this is said to have occurred on

one occasion when preaching to a riotous rabble of drunken and rollicking sailors. At the time one of the most popular ballads amongst seafaring men was a song called "Nancy Dawson." The tune and metre suited the jovial and dancing tendencies of British tars, and with this song they completely put a stop to his discourse. Shortly after he went to the same place again, and a similar scene was about to be repeated, when he gave out the following lines, which he had composed to the above named tune. The rough sailors caught the sound and were completely "brought to" by this device, and the service went on in peace.*

* The following are the lines above referred to. They have undergone some alteration from the original words, a copy of which may be found in the Methodist Magazine for 1834.

Listed in the cause of sin, Why should a good be evil?
Music, alas! too long hath been, Prest to obey the devil.
Drunken, or lewd, or light the lay Flowed to the soul's undoing,
Widened and strewed with flowers the way, Down to eternal ruin.

Come, let us try if Jesu's love, Will not as well inspire us;
This the theme of those above, This upon earth shall fire us.
Say, if your hearts are tuned to sing, Is there a subject greater?
Harmony all its strains may bring, Jesus' name is sweeter.

Who has a right like us to sing, Us whom his mercy raises?
Merry our hearts for Christ is king, Cheerful are all our faces.
Who of his love doth once partake, He evermore rejoices;
Melody in our hearts we make, Melody in our voices.

K

We will now proceed to notice some of the
hymns of the Rev. Charles Wesley, which appear in the present Hymn Book, and also give
some interesting facts illustrative of the same.

Hymn 1.   O for a thousand tongues to sing.

This is a noble opening song of praise and
triumph, and is the real key note to all that
follow.   It was originally called " The anniversary day of one's conversion," and consisted
of eighteen verses, the ten retained being
decidedly the best.   It was probably written on
the anniversary of the conversion of either John
or Charles.   The first line 'O for a thousand
tongues to sing,' is supposed to have been
suggested by the words of Peter Bohler, who in
a conversation with the poet about the Saviour,
said, " Had I a thousand tongues I would
praise him with them all."   A well known
preacher on one occasion when giving out this
hymn, after reading the first two lines, paused
and said to the congregation, " Listen ! listen !!
I say, friends, listen ! ! ! here's a man that wants

Then let us in His praises join, Triumph in His salvation,
Glory ascribe to love divine, Worship and adoration.
Heaven already is begun,   Opened in each believer;
Only believe and still go on, Heaven is ours for ever.

999 tongues besides his own to praise God with." Few men ever quoted passages from the Hymn Book with greater effect than the late William Dawson. On one occasion when preaching his celebrated sermon on Death on the White Horse, he gave out this hymn, and on coming to the eighth verse, he paused and said, "Come, and see! What? I do not ask you to come and see the preacher, to hear the voice of thunder, but to come and see *yourselves*, *your Sins*, and YOUR SAVIOUR, 'See all your sins on Jesus laid.'" The effect of this little incident was such as only those who have heard the far famed "Billy Dawson" can appreciate and understand.

Hymn 21. Ye simple souls that stray.

This hymn has been ascribed to both John and Charles Wesley. Mr. Kirk attaches to it both names, others think it belongs to Charles. The Rev. H. Moore, in his Life of Wesley gives it to John. The general opinion now is in favour of the latter. It was undoubtedly written on one of the many occasions of violent persecution through which both the brothers had to pass, but which we are unable to say.

In order to understand several of its allusions
it is necessary to become acquainted with some
of those scenes of brutal and fiendish violence.
The heroism and bravery of the writer of these
lines can be only then appreciated as we see him
confronting the raging multitude and throwing
back upon them the following words.

> So wretched and obscure,
> The men whom ye despise,
> So foolish, impotent, and poor,
> Above your scorn we rise.

The last four lines are very striking.   Imagine
a poor brother in the lowliest condition, living
in a cellar, in some back yard, clothed in tattered
garments, and fed on parish pay, singing,

> On all the kings of earth,
> With pity *I look down.*

Paradoxical and absurd as this may sound in
the ears of those whose notions of elevation
consist only in wealth and high stations ; yet
in the best of senses it is true.   Dr. Young
says, " A Christian is the *highest* style of man."
Religion raises a man far above kings and
princes, and puts him in possession of a claim
to a " never fading crown."

Hymn 30.   Where shall my wondering soul begin?

This hymn is supposed by many to be the
one written immediately after Charles Wesley's
conversion, and alluded to in his Journal, May
23rd, 1738, where he says, "At nine I began a
hymn on my conversion, but was persuaded to
break off for fear of pride.   Mr. Bray coming in
encouraged me to proceed in spite of Satan.   I
prayed Christ to stand by me, and finished the
hymn.   Upon my afterwards showing it to Mr.
Bray, the devil threw in a fiery dart, suggesting
that it was wrong, and I had displeased God.
My heart sunk within me, when, casting my
eye upon a Prayer Book, I met with an answer
for him.   "Why boasteth thou thyself, thou
tyrant, that thou canst do mischief."   Upon this
I clearly discovered it was a device of the enemy to keep back glory from God."

The Mr. Bray alluded to in the above para-
graph was the same individual as is mentioned
on the Title Page of the second volume of
Hymns published by Hutton,   "and sold at
Mr. Bray's, a brazier, in Little Britain."   Bray
was a pious, zealous man, for whom the poet
cherished a great esteem.   He says of him, " I
was just going to remove to old Mr. Hutton's,

when God sent Mr. Bray to me, a poor igno-
rant mechanic, who knows nothing but Christ,
yet by knowing Him, knows and discerns all
things."

Hymn 34.   Let heaven and earth agree.

This was a great favorite of the late John
Preston of Yeadon, near Leeds, better known
in that locality as " Joan Preston," a popular
and eccentric local preacher in his day.   Who
that ever knew "Oud Joan" can forget his fine,
tall, broad, and stalwart form, with his genial
face, and mighty voice, and his touching sket-
ches of death-bed visits, and the dying scenes
which he had witnessed ?   Who can forget his
strokes of humour, his shafts of irony, or his
powerful appeals to the consciences of sinners,
all delivered in the richest, broadest Yorkshire
dialect ?   Or who that was accustomed to hear
him thirty years ago on some village anniversary, can forget him, when, with form erect, and
looking towards the singers, he addressed them
as he opened the service, saying, " Nah lads,
Trumpet length !—   .

> Let airth and heaven agree,
> Aingils and men be joined."

Hymn 37. Jesus the Name high over all.

This is a noble and triumphant hymn, and
a great favourite in revival prayer meetings.
Almost every verse has some interesting fact
associated with it. A remarkable one in connection with the first is mentioned in the life of
the Rev. H. Ranson, given in the Methodist
Magazine for 1857. When Mr. Ranson laboured in the Wednesbury circuit, he was requested
to visit a young woman said to be possessed by
an "evil spirit,". He at first deemed the case
one of religious monomania and declined to go,
but at length went. He found the person in
great agony of mind, and the room filled with
people. After certain enquiries, he ascertained
that the visitation was of a most extraordinary
character, and evidently satanic. When the
sentence was uttered, " Jesus Christ shall cast
thee out, thou unclean spirit !" an unearthly
reply was given, " No he shall not," which was
followed by vollies of horrid imprecations. Mr.
Ranson soon perceived how completely the evil
one had taken possesion of her soul, and began
to take steps to effect her deliverance. For this
purpose he commenced giving out this hymn,
intending afterwards to wrestle in prayer on

her behalf. But whilst singing the first lines the snare was broken, the evil one departed, and she burst into rapture and praise, after which she fell into a deep sleep from which she awoke not for a long time.

An old Missionary from Ceylon, once told the writer that the converted natives were accustomed to sing this hymn, which was a great favourite amongst them, to the tune of "Crown Him Lord of all," and that he could not express the mingled sensations which he felt of the ludicrous and undevout, while they sung the last line of the first verse, "*And devils fear and fly*," the repetition resting upon the word "devils," repeating this word three or four times, ascending a note at each repetition as the tune requires, the dark distorted countenances of the natives, and their shrill unmusical voices in the mean time adding to the peculiarity of the scene, rendered it one that could not readily be forgotten.

Hymn 40.   Ye neighbours and friends, to Jesus draw near.

These words were composed after preaching to the colliers of Newcastle upon Tyne in 1746. The power of converting grace was strikingly

displayed in the awakening of thousands of the
vilest of the vile. While he preached the
divine breath swept over the masses of dry
bones and quickened them into life. The
words, the scenes which they depict, and the
bold and swelling measure in which the lines
are written, all are characteristic of those days
when "the word of the Lord mightily grew
and prevailed."

Hymn 44. And am I only born to die.

Mr. Dawson was once giving out this hymn,
when he introduced it by saying, "This is a
solemn and remarkable hymn, unlike most of
those we sing. It is neither a hymn of praise,
of adoration, nor yet of prayer. It is a soliloquy,
and represents a person talking to himself."
He then went on to say, "Let each person in
the congregation talk to himself, as I purpose
talking to myself, while we sing these solemn
words."

The following interesting fact is said to have
taken place in connection with this hymn. A
nobleman had a daughter who was the idol of
his heart. She was highly accomplished and
amiable, but a stranger to God. She was led

L

to attend a Methodist place of worship, was awakened and converted, and became a happy christian. The change was marked by her fond father with the utmost concern, who resolved to draw her away from what he considered an awful delusion. He furnished her with large sums of money, took her on long journeys, and endeavoured to throw her into gay company, in order to banish religion from her mind, and alienate her from the Methodist people. But amidst it all she maintained her integrity. It was arranged by her father that several young ladies should be invited to his house, and sing songs accompanied by the piano-forte. Several had performed their part, when she was called upon for her song. It was a moment of intense struggle. Should she decline she would be disgraced in her father's eyes. Should she comply, the enemy of her soul would triumph. Looking to God for help, she took her seat at the piano, and sung the verse commencing,

No room for mirth or trifling here.

She arose from her seat, the whole company was subdued. Her father wept aloud, and never rested until he became a true christian.

Hymn 46. Come, let us anew Our journey pursue.

This is the celebrated Watch-night hymn, which never seems to be in season, excepting at that solemn service. How intimately associated is this dear old hymn with all our Methodistic reminiscences. For a long, long series of years, these words have been the first to escape our lips as we have risen from our knees and welcomed the dawn of another new year. Many who now read these pages have often joined in this solemn midnight song; some probably have never missed a Watch-night since they started for heaven. Let such be thankful for so many mercies. God grant that we may all go on singing it until we are brought to that happy state where there will be "no more night," and where "rolling years shall cease to move."

There were other hymns written for the Watch-night services, but the rousing and elevating tune to which this is sung, and its remarkable adaptation to the season, have rendered it a universal favourite amongst the Methodist people in all parts of the world.*

* Watch-nights had their origin in a somewhat singular manner. In Crowther's Portraiture of Methodism we read, " 1742, The first

Hymn 52. Again we lift our voice.

O, what light and comfort has this sweet
hymn afforded in the dark and painful hour of
bereavement. As the coffin rested in the house,
or outside the door, containing the remains of
some devoted christian, and just before departing to the last resting place, old class mates and
christian friends have joined to sing—

> Our friend is gone before,
> To that celestial shore,
> He hath left his mates behind,
> He hath all the storm outrode,
> Found the rest we toil to find,
> Landed in the arms of God.

Hymn 57. The great archangel's trump shall sound.

The title of this hymn was, "After deliver-

Watch-night was held in London. The custom originated with the
colliers of Kingswood, near Bristol, who had been in the habit, when
slaves of sin, of spending every Saturday at the ale house. They now
devoted that night to prayer and singing of hymns. Mr. Wesley,
hearing of this, and of the good that was done, resolved to make it
general. At first he ordered *Watch-nights* to be kept once a month,
when the moon was at the full, and afterwards fixed them for once a
quarter."

Dr. Southey says, "The reclaimed colliers having been accustomed
to sit late on Saturday nights at the ale house, transferred their weekly
meetings after their conversion to the School house, and continued
there praying and *singing hymns far into the morning.*"

ance from death by the fall of an house." It
originally contained five or six more verses.
For a long account of this alarming circumstance, and extraordinary escape from destruction, we refer our readers to Charles Wesley's
Journal, under date March 14th, 1744, where
he gives a graphic description of the scene, and
finishes his record with the following words,"
" The news was soon spread through the town,
and drew many to the place, who expressed
their compassion by *wishing all our necks had
been broke.*"

Hymn 59.   Thou God of glorious majesty.

This is a solemn and impressive call to the
contemplation of the day of judgment, and
was originally called "An hymn for serious-
ness." The second verse, "Lo! on a narrow
neck of land," has a special interest in it. These
words refer to a remarkable spot at the Land's
End in Cornwall.   Dr. Adam Clarke visited
this place in 1819, and wrote the following
description of it.   "I write this on the last
projecting point of the Land's End : upwards
of 200 feet perpendicularly above the sea, which
is raging and roaring tremendously, threatening

destruction to myself and the narrow point of rock on which I am sitting. On my right hand is the British Channel, and before me the vast Atlantic Ocean. There is not one inch of land from the place on which my feet rest, to the American Continent. This is the place where Charles Wesley composed those fine lines, 'Lo! on a narrow neck of land.' The point of rock is about three feet broad at its termination, and the fearless adventurer will here place his foot to be able to say that he has been on the uttermost inch of land in the British Empire, westward."

This hymn has become permanently associated with this place all the world over. A bishop of the Church of England some time ago paid a visit to this celebrated rock, his conductor on the occasion was a Methodist. In describing the locality the good man said, "It was here that Mr. Wesley wrote his hymn." "What hymn?" said the bishop. The guide repeated a portion of it. "Did Mr. Wesley compose that?" exclaimed his lordship. "Yes," said the man, "did you not know?" surprised at such ignorance in a bishop.

Hymn 61. Stand the omnipotent decree.

Dr. Southey, the Poet Laureate, pronounced this to be "the finest lyric in the English language." It is remarkable for the similarity of expression between some portions of it and a passage in Young's Night Thoughts.

> Let this earth dissolve, and blend
> In death the wicked and the just ;
> Let those ponderous orbs descend,
> And grind us into dust.

Dr. Young's words are,

> " If so decreed, the Almighty will be done,
> Let earth dissolve, yon pond'rous orbs descend
> And grind us into dust."

Hymn 62. How happy are the little flock.

This and the two following were written in 1755, when the city of Lisbon was nearly destroyed by an earthquake,* and this country

---

* This terrible calamity awakened universal sympathy in this country. The British Parliament, to its honour, generously voted £100,000 towards relieving the necessities of the inhabitants. The following affecting circumstance took place in connection with this appalling event. An English gentleman of the name of Harboyne, a banker in the city, had occasion to go into the country on the morning of the fatal day. As he was returning home, whilst descending a hill, he saw a large portion of the city engulphed and swallowed up in a few seconds, including his wife, his children, his home, and all his property.

was greatly disturbed by political commotions. At that time Great Britain was at war with France and Spain, our shores were threatened with invasion for the purpose of restoring the exiled house of Stuart to the throne. Such were the circumstances which called forth these sublime and impressive hymns. They show the strong patriotic feelings, as well as the loyalty and devotion which glowed in the writer's heart.

Hymn 67. How weak the thoughts, and vain.

This noble hymn was occasioned by an earthquake which occurred in and around London in 1750. John Wesley, in his Journal, says : " March 8th, 1750. This morning at a quarter to five, we had another shock of an earthquake far more violent than that of February 8th. I was just repeating my text when it shook the Foundery so violently that we all expected it would fall upon our heads." See Charles Wesley's Journal, April 5th, 1750. " The late earthquake," he says, " has found

The effect upon him, as may well be supposed, was such that he lost his reason. On arriving in this country his friends placed him in charge of a keeper at Eldwick hall, near Bingley, where he lived and died a chained and raving maniac.

me work enough. Yesterday I saw the Westminster end of the town full of coaches, and crowds flying out of the reach of Divine Justice, with astonishing precipitation. Their panic was caused by a poor madman's prophecy. Last night they were all to be swallowed up. The vulgar were in almost as great consternation as their betters. Most of them watched all night, multitudes in the fields and open places, several in their coaches ; many removed their goods. London looked like a sacked city. A lady, just stepping into her coach to escape, dropped down dead. Many came all night knocking at the Foundery door, and begging admittance for God's sake. Our people were calm and quiet as at another time." His active pen found full employment on this theme, for we find him publishing, " Hymns occasioned by the Earthquake, 1750," consisting of nineteen, two only of which are found in the present book, the 67th and 555th.* When we consider the frightful panic which pervaded all classes of the Metropolis, we see in striking contrast

* In an enlarged edition of "Hymns Occasioned by the Earthquake," published in 1756, hymns 63 and 64 are included, but are inserted as one.

M

how the despised Methodists remained calm
and confident amidst it all. "Our people," he
says, "were calm and quiet as at another time."
And whilst we picture to ourselves the terrified
multitude kicking and knocking at the door of
the old Foundery, and crying for admittance,
we look also upon the worshippers inside, and
can understand the feelings which inspired the
following stanza :

> A house we call our own,
> Which cannot be o'erthrown :
> In the general ruin sure,
> Storms and *Earthquakes* it defies ;
> Built immovably secure ;
> Built eternal in the skies.

Hymn 73. Away with our sorrow and fear.

During the last illness of the late Rev.
Robert Wood, some allusion being made to
the Great Exhibition, 1851, in which he always
evinced great interest, a hope was expressed
that in a short time his desire to visit it might
be gratified. He shook his head, and said,
"No ; I shall never see the Crystal Palace :
but reach the Hymn Book, and read the 73rd
hymn, and you will find that I shall not lose
much."

By faith we already behold,
  That lovely Jerusalem here;
Her walls are of jasper and gold,
  As crystal her buildings are clear."
      See Wes. Meth. Mag. May, 1854, p. 678.

Hymn 84. Come, O Thou all victorious Lord.

This was written when he was going to preach to the Portland quarry men in 1746. Portland, which is noted for its immense stone quarries, is about four miles from Weymouth, and is connected with the main land by a narrow strip of shingle. The peculiar nature of the work in which the men were engaged reminded him of the stony heartedness of the people in religious matters, and led him to sing,

Come, O Thou all victorious Lord,
  Thy power to us make known;
Strike with the hammer of Thy word,
  And break these hearts of stone.

Hymn 103. O that I could revere.

The second verse in this hymn contains an allusion to a circumstance mentioned in classic story. It is said that Dionysius, king of Sicily, was flattered by one of his courtiers named Damocles, who spoke in terms of wonder and

admiration of his monarch's grandeur and happiness. The king, to show him his mistake,
induced him to take upon himself for awhile
the charge of royalty, to which he readily consented.   But on taking his place upon the
throne, he beheld a naked sword glittering
above his head suspended by a single hair.
The sight of this instantly spread a cloud over
all his glory, and he earnestly begged to be re-
lieved of his perilous honours. The poet, whose
classic mind was perfectly familiar with this
incident, would recognize in it a figure of the
sword of God's justice and wrath hanging over
the head of an unconverted sinner, and he put
these words into his mouth when praying for
repentance,

> Show me the naked sword,
> Impending o'er my head.

The poet Cowley, long before Charles Wesley's day, introduced the same illustration into
one of his effusions in the following words,

> Ye feast, I fear, like Democles :
> If you, your eyes could upwards move,
> (But you I fear think nothing is above,)
> Ye would perceive by what a little thread,
> *The sword still hangs over your head.*

Hymn 109. Wretched, helpless, and distressed.

A Mr. John Priestly, of Bacup, who died a short time ago, was long a member of the Methodist society before he realized the sense of his acceptance with God. He was often sore distressed, and filled with darkness, doubts, and fears. Early one morning he woke up from a dream which had much disturbed him, in which the words *One hundred and ninth*, were strongly impressed upon his mind. He had no idea what they meant. Throughout the night the sentence, *a hundred and ninth*, *a hundred and ninth*, kept running through his mind. When he arose he opened his Bible and turned to the 109th Psalm, thinking it was that particular psalm he must have been dreaming about, but no, there was nothing in it suitable to his case. It then occurred to him to look at the 109th Hymn, which he found to describe his state of mind. He read it again, and again, until his soul which had been groaning in bondage for ten years, found liberty and peace, from which time until his death, he continued a happy christian.

Hymn 115. Let the world their virtue boast.

The last two lines of every verse in this

hymn have been more frequently quoted than any other portion of the hymn book. When the awakened and penitent sinner has felt his sense of guilt to be overpowering, and yet he has cherished hopes of mercy through a crucified Redeemer, no words have more suitably expressed his feelings than,

> " I the chief of sinners am,
> But Jesus died for me."

The two great doctrines, of the fall of man, and his redemption by Christ, being so distinctly and positively recognised in the couplet, we need not be surprised that an awakened conscience should find in it instinctive utterance. Good men too, who have felt their sense of sin to be great, and who have confessed themselves to be void and destitute of all merit, have found these words to be in perfect harmony with their feelings. Some of the most distinguished saints have fallen asleep in Jesus with these words upon their lips. John Wesley, a short time before he died, said, " How necessary it is to be on the right foundation,

> ' I the chief of sinners am,
> But Jesus died for me."

The venerable Henry Moore when dying, raised his hand as high as he could lift it, and exclaimed,

> " I the chief of sinners am,
> But Jesus died for me."

The Rev. David Macallum, a short time before he departed to his final rest, said, " My labours are done, but I build nothing on them, I build only on the merits of my Saviour, I feel that,

> ' I the chief of sinners am,
> But Jesns died for me.' "

Hymn 140. Come, O thou traveller unknown.

This is the celebrated hymn called " Wrestling Jacob," concerning which Dr. Watts said that it was worth all that he had ever written, and respecting which James Montgomery wrote that it was the " grandest achievement of lyric art." The pictures are most graphic. A sermon which the author had preached a short time before with great interest and power on the subject of Jacob's conflict with the angel, gave birth to this beautiful hymn. The intense struggle is vividly brought before us. " The absence of company, the night season, the length

of the struggle, the lameness inflicted on the
patriarch, the return of the morning, the com-
munication of the desired blessing, are all
brought to bear upon the penitent's deliverance
from sin, obtained by praying, agonising faith,
and followed by the joy of pardon and holiness."
What pathos and power there is in the second
verse!

I need not tell Thee who I am,
My misery and sin declare :
Thyself hast called me by my name,
Look on Thy hands and read it there ;
But who, I ask Thee, who art Thou?
Tell me Thy Name, and tell me now.*

* We cannot refrain from giving the following vivid and impressive
description of the conflict by the Rev. John Kirk, along with which
should be read the whole hymn.

"Night has drawn her curtain and gained her noon. Flocks and
herds quietly rest on their grassy lair. The streamlet which many
years ago the solitary wanderer has crossed with his staff, murmurs
its midnight music. The fervent prayer to the God of Abraham is
finished, its last echoes have died away. The suppliant, lone and
weary, has risen from his knees with thoughts intent upon that
morrow which is to exert so great an influence, for weal or for woe,
upon his entire future. His only hope is in the God of his fathers, and
he tremblingly awaits the issue. In that anxious moment, a form
unknown stands by his side. A hand, strong in its resolute grasp, is
upon his shoulder: and the mystic Visitant begins to wrestle with
him, as if by some sudden assault he would fling him to the ground.
* * * * In that struggle he obtains a blessing above all price, and
wins a new name which beautifully symbolises the inward and spiritual change.

Hymn 143.   Jesu, lover of my soul.

This is a universal favourite, and both in
depth of feeling, and prayerful looking up to
Christ in human feebleness, may be considered
a companion hymn to " Rock of Ages, cleft for
me."   In the esteem of many the former holds
the pre-eminence.   It is adapted to the experience of God's people amidst the varied
exigences and trials of life.   Many a heart,
bleeding, broken, and crushed by accumulated
sorrows, has found relieving utterance in these
words ; and many a suffering, dying saint has
finished his mortal voyage, and entered into
the haven of rest with these words upon his
lips.   In the estimation of a learned, but hostile,
critic, " Jesu, lover of my soul," is of itself
amply sufficient to stamp its author, had he
written nothing else, with the character of a
hymnist of the highest class.   But the best
proofs of its preciousness are to be found in the
daily experience of God's people.

Not long ago a sailor was observed in the
rigging of a shipwrecked vessel without the
means of escape.   While the ship was sinking,
and amid the crisis of the wreck, he was heard
singing,

N

> Jesu, lover of my soul,
>   Let me to Thy bosom fly,
> While the nearer waters roll,
>   While the tempest still is high.

And as the vessel gradually settled down, and sank in the waste of waters, he continued singing,

> Hide me, O my Saviour hide,
>   Till the storm of life be past ;
> Safe into the haven guide,
>   O receive my soul at last !

Thus closing his eyes in death, he no doubt passed away to heaven.

A few years ago an emigrant vessel left the shores of England. Soon after her departure a fire broke out which resulted in the destruction of the ship, and the loss of many of those on board. One family, consisting of husband, wife, and child, was wonderfully preserved. In the confusion, the husband was taken away from the side of his wife ; and in her distress, as the flames rapidly approached, she bound her child to her bosom and plunged into the ocean, prefering a watery grave to death by fire. In doing so she fell upon a portion of the wreck which was floating near. Onwards they drifted, until at length something was seen by the crew of a distant vessel bound to America, who launched their boat and hastened to discover what it was. As they approached they heard the sound of a human voice. They listened as they rested on their oars, when, to their surprise, they heard a female voice plaintively singing, and the words which fell upon their ears were those of this beautiful hymn,

> Hide me, O my Saviour hide,
> Till the storm of life be past ;
> Safe into the haven guide,
> O receive my soul at last !

The wrecked ones were speedily delivered from their perilous position. On reaching the shores of America friendless, and, as she supposed, a widow, judge of her surprise and pleasure, when on landing, she fell into the arms of her beloved husband, who, after being preserved in a similar manner to his wife and child, but having arrived first, was anxiously watching the arrival of some vessel, which he hoped might bring tidings of his loved ones.

Hymn 147.   O Love divine, how sweet Thou art.

The last verse of this hymn once afforded Mr. Dawson an opportunity of showing his

peculiar force in giving out our hymns. After
the former verses had been sung with great
liveliness and spirit, he came to the last three
lines, "Now," said he, " pay attention to the
next, you have in them a remarkable gradation,
the sense rising higher and stronger with every
word." He commenced in a low tone, and then
increasing his voice with each succeeding word,
until he reached the last sentence, he filled the
chapel with one of his loudest shouts;—

> My only *Care*, *Delight*, and *Bliss*,
> My *Joy*, my *Heaven on Earth*, be this,
> To hear the Bridegroom's voice.

The face of Mr. Dawson must have been
seen, and his strong stentorian voice heard, to
realise anything like an idea of the impression
and power of such a circumstance.

Hymn 160. O Jesus, my hope, for me offered up.

The two first lines of the third verse of this
hymn received a striking and beautiful illustration in the following circumstance.

In a mining district, a young girl who was
employed in breaking ore, became a follower of
Christ. As she was busy one day in her usual

avocation, some one reproached her on account of the ear-rings which she wore, saying they proved her hypocrisy and pride. She immediately removed them, and with the hammer she was using broke them to pieces, singing as she did so,

Neither passion nor pride, Thy cross can abide,
But melt in the fountain that streams from Thy side.

Hymn 168. Depth of mercy, can there be.

This is one of Charles Wesley's choicest productions. When the soul is overwhelmed with mingled emotions of shame and sorrow, and is filled with a mournful sense of its ingratitude and sinfulness, what words express its feelings more suitably than the first four lines of this hymn? Reader, have you not often proved them so in your experience? The following interesting circumstance is recorded as having transpired in connection with this hymn. An actress in one of the principal theatres, was one day passing through the streets, when her attention was arrested by the sound of voices proceeding from a cottage. Looking in, she saw a few poor people, one of whom was giving out the following lines,

" Depth of mercy, can there be," which the
others joined in singing. The words rivetted
her attention, and she stood motionless until
she was invited to enter, which she did, and
was much affected by the service. She quitted
the cottage, but the words of the hymn followed
her, and she resolved to procure the book
which contained the hymn, the hearing of
which led her to give her heart to God. The
manager of the theatre, not knowing the great
change she had undergone, called upon her as
usual to request her to perform in a new
play for his benefit, the next week. She
declined, he appealed and urged her to comply,
and she at length consented. On the night of
performance she made her appearance upon
the stage under deep emotion, and after a long
pause, with hands clasped, and eyes suffused
with tears, she sang not the song announced
upon the bills, but this beautiful hymn,

> Depth of mercy, can there be,
> Mercy still reserved for me ?

The sensation was immense, and the play was
brought to a close. She maintained her stead-
fastness, and afterwards became the wife of a

minister of the gospel. Little did those few
humble Methodists, for no doubt such they
were, little did they think when singing in that
prayer meeting those well known words, that
God would make them the means of producing
such results.

Hymn 201. And can it be that I should gain.

This is considered by many to be what is
called his "conversion hymn," that is, the one
he wrote to celebrate the passing of his soul
out of darkness into light. And certainly none
could be more appropriate, especially the joyful
and triumphant language of the last verse,

No condemnation now I dread,
Jesus, and all in Him, are mine.

Hymn 202. Arise, my soul, arise.

In Roman history we have an account of an
insurrection in which a most affecting circumstance is narrated. Two brothers, devotedly
attached to each other, took directly opposite
parts in the outbreak, the elder one siding with
the government, and the younger with the
rebel party. In the conflict the former lost both
his arms, the latter was taken prisoner, placed

on his trial, and sentence of death was just about to be passed upon him. At this instant a sensation ran through the court. The judge demanded to know the reason of it. No one could inform him. But a wounded man came forward, and held up before the judge his still-bleeding stumps. No words were uttered, but there he stood in solemn silence. It was soon ascertained that he was the brother of the guilty man. The judge was overwhelmed with emotion ; he looked upon the pleader and then upon the rebel, and after a solemn pause, he pardoned the one for the sake of what the other had done and suffered for his country. And does not Jesus Christ, our elder brother, plead on our behalf, and show His wounds to God for us ? This beautiful incident reminds us of the third verse of this hymn,

Five bleeding wounds He bears,
Received on Calvary,
They pour effectual prayers,
They strongly speak for me ;
" Forgive Him, O forgive," they cry,
" Nor let that ransom'd sinner die !"

Hymn 203.   Glory to God, whose sovereign grace.

This hymn is descriptive of the wonderful

work of God accomplished by the preaching of the gospel amongst the Kingswood colliers. Its original title was, "Hymn for the Kingswood Colliers." These men had long been notorious for blasphemy, lewdness, profane singing, and drunkenness. But a mighty change was wrought in many of their hearts. With this knowledge of their previous habits we see the appropriateness of the words which Charles Wesley put into their lips, especially such as the following :

> Suffice that for the season past,
>   Hell's horrid language filled our tongue,
> We all Thy words behind us cast,
>   And lewdly sang the drunkard's song.
> But, O, the power of grace divine !
>   In hymns we now our voices raise,
> Loudly in strange hosannas join,
>   And blasphemies are turned to praise !

Charles Wesley mentions in his Journal a circumstance characteristic of these men. The wife of one of them had given her heart to God and joined the Methodist society. While I was praying" says Mr. W. "a wild collier brought me four of his children, and threw the youngest on the table before me, crying, 'You have got the mother, take the bairns too.'"

O

Hymn 205. My God I am Thine, What a comfort divine.

This hymn possesses an interest from the following circumstance in connection with the conversion of the Rev. Joseph Entwistle, the elder.   When under deep concern about his soul and anxiously seeking salvation, a pious young man said to him one day as they were walking together to the house of God. "Joseph, I will read you a hymn which those of us sing *who know our sins forgiven.*"   He then opened his hymn book, and read this beautiful hymn. He was much struck with it, not having heard or read it before, and expressed an ardent desire to be enabled to adopt its language as descriptive of his own experience.   Soon after this he found the blessing which he sought, and his biographer says, " He was able to sing with joy unspeakable the beautiful hymn on adoption already referred to, and which, being associated in his mind with deeply interesting recollections, became a favourite hymn with him to the day of his death."

Hymn 218. See how great a flame aspires.

This was written after visiting Newcastle upon Tyne. The first verse was suggested, it is supposed, by the numerous colliery and furnace fires which abound in that neighbourhood. As he gazed upon them blazing forth in the darkness, on the hill sides, or in the valleys, he saw the love of God like a fire spreading amongst the people, and prayed that

> All might catch the flame,
> All partake the glorious bliss.

Hymn 219, All thanks be to God.

This was written to commemorate the marvellous outpouring of the Spirit at Gwennap in 1746. In his Journal he says, " Nine or ten thousand listened with all eagerness while I commended them to God, and faith in Jesus Christ. I broke out again and again in prayer and exhortation. Seventy years of suffering were overpaid by one such opportunity. * * * I expressed the gratitude of my heart in the following thanksgiving,

> All thanks be to God,
> Who scatters abroad."

Hymn 228. Thou Shepherd of Israel and mine.

This was the late Dr. Hannah's favourite hymn, which he greatly admired. It was repeated to him, probably at his request, a short time before he departed to his heavenly rest; and was sung with deep emotion by a vast audience at the close of his funeral sermon, preached in Manchester by the President of the Conference. Who that knew Dr. Hannah does not recognise between the man and this beautiful hymn a close and striking resemblance?

Hymn 229.   God of my life, to Thee.

The two last lines of this hymn are supposed to refer to Deut, xxxiv., where we read, " So Moses the servant of the Lord died there in the land of Moab, *according to the word of the Lord*." From the last sentence the Jews derived a tradition that God with a kiss of his divine lips drew away to heaven the soul of his faithful servant. The poet asks for a similar favour when he sings,

Like Moses to Thyself convey,
And kiss my raptured soul away.

Dr. Watts introduces the same tradition into his hymn, " On the death of Moses,"

Softly his fainting head he lay
Upon his Maker's breast;
His Maker *kissed his soul away*,
And laid his flesh to rest.

Hymn 230. Fountain of life, and all my joy.

This and the following, and the one preceding, were written to celebrate his own birthday.
It originally contained ten verses each of which
ended, as those in the book do, with the grateful and hearty expression,

Though in the flesh I bear the thorn,
I bless the day that I was born.

Hymn 247. Holy as Thou, O Lord is none.

Mr. J. Wesley was once holding a lovefeast
at the Foundery when an elderly man rose to
speak. He stated that he had lately been
favoured with a remarkable work of grace in
his soul, and that he had become as pure and
holy as God himself. On resuming his seat,
Mr. W. rose and said, " God has given our
brother a new heart, but not a new head." Mr.
Charles Wesley, on hearing of this incident,
called for pen and ink, and wrote this hymn,
founded on 1 Sam. ii. 2.

Holy as Thou, O Lord, is none !
Thy holiness is all Thy own ;
A drop of that unbounded sea
Is ours, a drop derived from Thee.

And when Thy purity we share,
Thy only glory we declare ;
And, humbled into nothing, own
Holy and pure is God alone !

Hymn 262.   A thousand oracles divine.

The late Rev. W. J. Shrewsbury ascribed
his deliverance from the bondage of sin, and the
possession of conscious pardon, to the singing
of this hymn. He says in his journal, "Dec. 27,
(1814,) was the day of liberty to my soul.   At
half-past eight in the evening, while singing
that hymn, ' A thousand oracles divine,' I came
to these lines,—

'And the whole Trinity descends
Into our faithful hearts.'

I felt the Lord had taken possession of my soul,
my doubts all fled away, and I was enabled to
rejoice in God my Saviour." Another interesting fact in his life was closely connected with
this hymn.   His call to the ministry was attended with great exercises of mind and sore
temptations, from which he experienced a glorious deliverance.   He says, " I went to the
watch-night.   In the course of the evening I
had to exhort, I ascended the pulpit and gave

out, 'Arise, my soul, arise!' Faith seemed at
that instant to spring up in my heart, and
whilst delivering a short exhortation my heart
was like melting wax, so that I could scarcely
speak. When I came down from the pulpit,
that hymn was given out,

'A thousand oracles divine,'

when we came to those lines,

'And the whole Trinity descends
Into our faithful hearts.'

God seemed to bow the heavens and come
down, and the Trinity descended into my long
unbelieving soul. I could scarcely refrain from
crying out in the congregation. I stood leaning
against the pew with my handkerchief before
my face, while my eyes overflowed with tears
of gratitude and love."

Hymn 272. Peace, doubting heart, my God's I am.

The Rev. John Wesley makes use of the
second verse of this hymn on a somewhat
adventurous and dangerous occasion. He says,
" Sept. 12th, 1743. I had for some time a
great desire to go and publish the love of God
our Saviour, if it were but for one day, in the

Isles of Scilly. This evening three of the brethren came and offered to carry me, if I could procure the Mayor's boat, which they said was the best sailer in the town. I sent, and he lent it me immediately, So the next morning, (the 13th,) John Nelson, Mr. Shepherd, and I, with three men and a pilot, sailed from St. Ives. It seemed strange to me to attempt going in a fisher boat, fifteen leagues upon the main ocean; especially when the waves began to swell, and hang over our heads. But I called to my companions, and we all joined together in singing lustily, and with a good courage,

> When passing through the watery deep,
>   I ask in faith His promised aid.
> The waves an awful distance keep,
>   And shrink from my devoted head,
> Fearless their violence I dare,
> They cannot harm, for God is there.

About half an hour after one, we landed, on St. Mary's, the chief of the inhabited islands."

Hymn 276. Worship, and thanks, and blessing.

The title of this hymn was, "Written after a deliverance in a tumult." One of the most furious outbursts of persecution which Charles Wesley had to endure occurred in 1747, at Devizes, a long account of which may be found in the first volume of his Journal. He writes, " Feb. 24th. Between three and four in the afternoon I came to Mr. Clark's, at Devizes. * * * We soon perceived that our enemies had taken the alarm, and were mustering their forces for the battle. They began with ringing the bells backwards, and running to and fro in the streets as lions roaring for their prey." The storm raged all that day, and was continued on the next with greater violence. He writes, " Wed. Feb. 25th. A day never to be forgotten ! " And so the reader will think if he turns to the record in the Journal. Amongst many displays of brutal and fiendish hatred, he says, " Such fierceness and diabolical malice I have not seen in human faces. * * * * After riding two or three hundred yards, I looked back, and saw Mr. Meriton on the ground in the midst of the mob and two bull-dogs upon him." For a full account of these proceedings we refer the reader to Mr. C. Wesley's Journal. The narrative closes thus, "We joined in hearty praise to our deliverer, singing the hymn,

P

Worship, and thanks, and blessing."

From the last sentence it is evident that this hymn was not written on the occasion of the Devizes persecution, as has been often supposed, but was then already in existence. Some previous outburst had inspired it.

Hymn 310. Into a world of ruffians sent.

Charles Wesley had many proofs of the truthfulness of the first verse of this hymn. Amongst the numerous instances of his escape from the hands of robbers and brutal persecutors, he mentions the following. "I set out for London. In a mile's riding my horse fell lame. I sung the 91st Psalm and put myself under divine protection. I had scarce ended, and turned the hut on Shotover hill, when a man came up to me, and demanded my money, showing, but not presenting a pistol. I gave him my purse. He asked how much there was. "About thirty shillings." "Have you no more?" "I will see;" put my hand in my pocket, and gave him some halfpence. He repeated the question, "Have you any more?" I had thirty pounds in a private pocket; bade him search myself; which he did not choose.

He ordered me to dismount, which I did; but
begged hard for my horse again, promising not
to pursue him. He took my word and restored
him. I rode gently on praising God. My bags,
and watch, and gold, the robber was *forced* to
leave me. By the evening I reached Westminster."

Hymn 327. O Thou who camest from above.

This was a great favourite with the late Dr.
Newton, and was frequently sung in family
devotion, especially on Saturday evenings. And
one more suitable to prepare him for his sab-
bath labours could not be found. When on his
voyage to America as the Representative of
the British Conference, he says, " We had
prayers in the ladies' cabin and sang, ' O Thou
who camest from above,' how I was reminded
of sweet home." On his return from his mis-
sion a large gathering of his family united in
singing this old familiar hymn. A few days
before his death he attempted to repeat these
lines, but his giant strength was gone, his arti-
culation failed him. Before that week was out
the last two lines were triumphantly realised in
the following dying sentences which fell from

his lips, "I am going to leave you, but God will be with you, farewell; I am going to join the myriads of angels and archangels before the throne of God. Farewell sin, and farewell death. Praise the Lord. Praise him for ever."

This hymn was also a great favorite of John Wesley. The Rev. S. Bradburn, when relating a conversation which he had with him, says, "He told me that his experience might almost at any time be found in this hymn."

Hymn 334. Lord, I adore Thy gracious will.

This brief hymn, consisting of but one verse, was written on 2 Sam. xvi. 10, which records the bitter curses heaped on David by Shimei. It embodies the high principle of christian forbearance, and teaches us to recognise in the "complicated wrongs" of men, the "kind rebukes" of God. A remarkable case of this sort is mentioned in the life of the Rev. Joseph Entwisle. He says, "A trial of a singular nature arose to day. A young man who was once my most intimate friend, is become my most implacable enemy. For years together we met in band, we took sweet counsel together, and went to the house of God in company.

Yea, we were so closely united, that we were almost like the primitive christians who had all things common. Thus we continued to live in the closest habits of friendship, till, about two years after I began to travel, he fell from God." Mr. E. goes on to describe how this individual became an idle dishonest vagabond, and a furious and malignant persecutor of his friend, the enmity he cherished leading him to circulate the foulest reports in those places where Mr. Entwisle had to preach. The trial was a most bitter one indeed, as several passages in his memoir will show. " My mind is exceedingly depressed," he writes, " on account of the present trial, and the enemy harasses me so with representing *what may be*, in the most dreadful colours, that I can scarcely bear the burden of it." But, says he, " the Lord will preserve me from evil."

> Lord, I adore Thy gracious will;
> Through every instrument of ill
>   My Father's goodness see ;
> Accept the complicated wrong
> Of Shimei's hand and Shimei's tongue,
>   As kind rebukes from Thee !

Hymn 335. Cast on the fidelity.

This and the 336th were composed for a female about to be confined, probably his own wife. The title was, " For a woman near the time of her delivery." If read with this fact borne in mind, the peculiar appropriateness of many of the allusions will be understood. Many a mother will appreciate the beautiful and tender representation of her sufferings and fears during those trying times, and know what those words mean in such circumstances,—

<blockquote>
Better than my boding fears.
</blockquote>

Hymn 477.   Father, Son, and Holy Ghost.

This is a hymn for the baptism of adults which Dr. Clarke used with so much effect on the public baptism of two young Brahmin priests, who had been sent over to England to be educated, and had been converted to christianity mainly through his instrumentality. In the presence of an immense Liverpool congregation, on Sunday, March 12th, 1820, the doctor performed the rite of baptism, on which occasion this hymn was sung. On coming to the fifth and sixth lines,

<blockquote>
See these sinful worms of earth !
Bless to them the cleansing flood !
</blockquote>

He proceeded to lay his hands upon their heads, when the young priests burst into tears as they listened to those words, and the vast assembly was thrilled with awe and intense emotion.

Hymn 488. How happy are we, Who in Jesus agree.

This hymn was written for social interviews among christian friends. Its original title was, " Written to be sung at the Tea table." It seems they loved and enjoyed a cup of tea in Charles Wesley's days, notwithstanding the high price of that article above a hundred years ago. It is a very cheerful and animated song, and we can easily picture to ourselves a company of joyful, hearty Methodists of the olden time, sitting round a table partaking of a refreshing cup of tea, and singing,

How pleasant and sweet, In his Name when we meet ;
Is His fruit to our spiritual taste.
We are banqueting here On angelical cheer,
And the joys that eternally last.

Hymn 491. Come away to the skies, My beloved arise.

This was composed to celebrate his wife's birthday. Few men were happier in their married state, or more tenderly attached to their wives, than Charles Wesley. Those frequent references in his Journal to his "dear Sally," and the loving letters which he frequently sent her when absent from home, all show how dearly he treasured her in his heart of hearts. It will require no great effort to picture him with his fine open countenance and glowing heart, entering the bed room of Mrs. Wesley on her birthday before she had risen, and singing,

> Come away to the skies, My beloved arise,
> And rejoice in the day thou wast born.

Hymn 645.   Blow ye the trumpet, blow.

This hymn was written for " New Year's Day." It has acquired a measure of interest from the fact of its being a special favourite of old John Brown, of Harper Ferry fame. It will be remembered that he was executed for his attempt by force to emancipate the slaves in the United States. His abhorrence of slavery was like a fire in his bones, and his love of freedom found congenial sentiments in this jubilant song. He inspired his children with the same feelings, several of whom fell in the same cause for which their brave old **father** died. He nursed them when young with the tenderness of a mother, and sang them to sleep with the words of this hymn. The love of freedom thus awakened led him and his sons to perish in the struggle. Yet, the unlooked for, but complete emancipation of the slaves, four or five years afterwards, proved the truth of those words of the song, which have been sung on so many. American battle-fields since his death,

> " John Brown's body lies mouldering in the ground,
>   His soul is marching on.
> He's gone to be a soldier in the army of the Lord,
>   His soul is marching on."

After his execution his body was given up to his friends, and conveyed to his home at North Elba, near the Adirondack mountains. His remains were laid in a rock which stands about fifty feet from the door of his own house, and which he had previously fixed upon to be his sepulchre. The funeral service was accompanied with the singing of this, his favourite hymn,

> " Blow ye the trumpet, blow."

Q

Hymn 675.   Away, my needless fears.

This hymn is intimately connected with the
late Dr. Newton and the lady who became his
faithful wife and widow.   The first time Mrs.
Newton saw her husband was when attending a
service at York.   She had previously resolved
to live a single life, but as she was engaged in
devotion with her eyes closed, it was impressed
upon her mind that if she there and then opened her eyes she would see the man who would
become her future husband.   After endeavour-
ing to repress the feeling, she at length yielded
to the conviction, when she saw "a tall young
man, attired in the style of an English yeoman."
After service she returned home without seeing
him again.   A day or two after she received an
invitation to attend a small party to tea at the
house of Mr. Burdsall, ("Dicky Burdsall.") in
York.   On arriving, to her great surprise, the
same figure stood before her amongst others.
Her mother, who had accompanied her, as
well as herself, was about retiring, when prayer
was proposed before they went.   "Let us sing
a hymn," said Mr. Newton, giving out, "Away
my needless fears," which he sang with the
others in his deep bass melodious voice, and

then offered prayer. This interview led to others, and ultimately to their long and happy union. The original heading of this hymn is, "In danger of losing friends;" but in Robert Newton's case it no doubt had considerable influence in gaining the most dear and precious companion of his days.

Hymn 681. Vain, delusive world, adieu.

Dr. Adam Clarke, when a youthful preacher, visited the village of Road, near Frome, where the cause was very low. A report got abroad that "a boy was going to preach in the Methodist chapel," which brought a crowd of young people to hear him. After preaching a powerful and impressive sermon, he gave out this hymn, which was sung with deep and thrilling emotion. He paused at the last verse, and said, "My dear young friends, you have joined with me heartily, and I dare say, sincerely, in singing this fine hymn. You know in whose presence we have been conducting this solemn service. The eyes of God, of angels, and perhaps of devils, have been upon us. And what have we been doing? We have been promising, in the sight of all these, and of each other, that we

will renounce a vain, delusive world, its plea-
sures, pomp, and pride, and seek our happiness
in God alone." He proceeded at some length
in this strain of earnest appeal and exhortation,
which resulted in a great awakening amongst
his hearers, and an extensive revival of the
work of God in that locality.

Hymn 733. How happy every child of grace.

This hymn, and the two following, are called
"Funeral Hymns," and are considered by com-
petent judges to be the finest odes of the kind
ever written. John Wesley pronounced them
to be much superior even to Wrestling Jacob.*
The Rev. Thomas Jackson says, "These three
exquisite compositions, for sweetness and spiri-
tuality were never surpassed." Mr. Burgess
says, "Had Charles Wesley composed nothing
but these three incomparable hymns, he would
have conferred a great and lasting benefit on
the Church of God, and would have immortal-
ised his name as a christian poet." At Exeter
Assizes, a few years ago, a most interesting and

* When speaking of Dr. Watts' well known words respecting his
opinion of Wrestling Jacob, Mr. Wesley once said, "O, what would
he have said if he had lived to see my brother's exquisite funeral
hymns!"

affecting circumstance took place in connection with hymn 733. A pious young female was brutally treated and left for dead. She rallied sufficiently to point out the guilty person, soon after which she died singing portions of this beautiful hymn. On the trial the counsel for the prosecution, with thrilling eloquence, narrated the death bed experience of the poor girl, reciting at the same time these triumphant lines, the effect of which was to melt the judge, the jury, and the court to tears.

TESTIMONIES OF DISTINGUISHED INDIVIDUALS TO THE VALUE AND USEFULNESS OF THE WESLEYAN HYMN BOOK.

THE REV. JOHN FLETCHER, of Madley, when the first edition was placed in his hands, said, in his broken English, "Dat book is de most valuable gift dat God has bestowed upon de Methodist Societies, next to de Bible."

DR. SOUTHEY, the Poet Laureate, says, "Perhaps no poems have been so devoutly committed to memory, nor quoted so often on a death-bed, as those of Charles Wesley,"

JAMES MONTGOMERY, the great Christian Poet, says, "As the Poet of Methodism, Charles Wesley has sung the doctrines of the gospel as they are expounded among that people. Christian experience, from the depths of affliction, through all the gradations of doubt, fear, desire, faith, hope, and expectation, to the transports of perfect love, in the very beams of the beatific vision ; he has celebrated these with an affluence of diction, and a splendour of colouring, rarely surpassed."

THE REV. RICHARD WATSON, says, "There is perhaps no uninspired book from which, as to the deep things of God, so much is to be learned, as from the Hymn Book in use in the Methodist congregations."

ISAAC TAYLOR, says, "It may be affirmed that there is no principal element of christianity, no main article of belief as professed by Protestant Churches, that there is no moral or ethical sentiments peculiarly characteristic of the gospel, that does not find itself emphatically and pointedly and clearly conveyed in some stanza of Charles Wesley's hymns."

DR. SANDWITH, says, when speaking of the Hymn Book, "It comes home to the heart in all its various religious emotions, and so adapts itself to every scene and circumstance of life, that the humble, as well as the more educated, have hymned it over the plough, the loom, the helm, and the dying pillow, in language the most elevated and spirit-stirring."

DR. STEVENS, in his beautiful and graphic History of Methodism, says, "The whole soul of Charles Wesley was imbued with poetic genius. His thoughts seemed to bask and revel in rhythm. The variety of his metres shows how impulsive were his poetic emotions, and how wonderful his facility in their spontaneous and varied utterance. They march at times like lengthened processions with solemn grandeur ; they sweep at other times like chariots of fire through the heavens ; they are broken like the sobs of grief

at the grave side; play like the joyful affections of childhood at the hearth; or shout like victors in the fray of the
battle field. No man ever surpassed Charles Wesley in the
harmonies of language. To him it was a diapason."

DR. DIXON says, "The hymns we sing embrace, we are
bold to affirm, one of the finest bodies of divinity extant;
as well as poetic beauty and sentiment, almost inimitable.
They enter into all the details of experience, the feelings of
the heart are touched with the tenderest pathos; and the
different stages of the life of God, from the first emotion of
penitent desire up to the highest raptures of sacred joy, and
pious, holy love, are described, and have an appropriate
medium of expression."

THE REV. PHILIP GARRET said during his last illness,
in reference to the Hymn Book, "That is the most blessed
uninspired book in the world."

MRS. CHARLES, in her work called "The voice of Christian Life in Song," when speaking of the Wesleyan Hymn
Book, says, "Those hymns are sung now in collieries and
copper mines. How many has their heavenly music strength-
ened to meet death in the dark coal pit; on how many
dying hearts have they come back, as from a mother's lips,
on the battle field; beside how many death beds have they
been chanted by trembling voices, and listened to with joy
unspeakable; how many have they supplied with prayer
and praise, from the first thrill of spiritual fear, to the last
rapture of heavenly hope. They echo along the Cornish
moors as the corpse of the christian miner is borne to his
last resting place; they cheer with heavenly messages the
hard bondage of slavery; they have been the first words of
thanksgiving on the lips of the liberated negro; they have
given courage to brave men, and patience to suffering

women ; they have been a liturgy engraven on the hearts of the poor ; they have borne the name of Jesus far and wide, and helped to write it deep on countless hearts, and England is no more without a People's Hymn Book."

We could have supplied other testimonies equally as high and strong, but our space obliges us to omit them.

———————◆———————

LET the reader, after going through these testimonies, turn to the preface of the Hymn Book and read over again the words of John Wesley written in 1779, respecting the high character of these hymns, and he will see in the quotations we have just given, how his words have been confirmed by the public declarations of some of the greatest and best of men, and that amidst the numerous *Selections*, and *Collections*, *Hymns* and *Psalms*, used by the various branches of the christian church, his *Collection of Hymns for the People called Methodists*, still holds the pre-eminence. And whose heart has not felt their power, and realised their excellence and preciousness ? Who that has ever sung them in the closet, the class meeting, the prayer meeting, or in public worship, will not add his own testimony to their worth ? What was once said concerning hymns in general has a peculiar force in reference to these. "Next to the Bible itself, these have done more to influence our views, and mould our theology, than any other instrumentality whatever. There is a power in hymns which never dies. Easily learned in the days of childhood and of youth, often repeated, seldom, if ever forgotten, they abide with us as a most precious heritage amid all the changes of our earthly life." In confirmation of these statements, we add the almost dying words of the celebrated Dr. Adam Clarke, which he wrote only seven weeks before his death. " I feel a simple heart. The prayers of my childhood are yet precious to me ; and *the simple hymns which I sang when a child, I sing now with unction and delight.*"

<hr />

WE must now bring our labours to a close. We have completed our tour of observation, and gone round and through the Wesleyan Hymn Book, according to the title of the work ; ROUND IT by sketching its history, and THROUGH IT by describing its contents, as stated in the preface. How we have performed the journey we must leave our readers to judge. We have endea-

R

voured to be as accurate as possible, but as the constant interruptions of an itinerant ministry interfere so greatly with the time and thought required for such a work, it is probable that a few errors will be found. On this ground, saying nothing of others, we ask the kind forbearance of our readers. It is with the utmost diffidence that we venture to publish this little work, and it is only at the earnest request of a considerable number of judicious friends, and a sincere desire to serve the church in this particular department, that we have been induced to do so. Unspeakably glad and thankful will the writer be if his object shall be gained, if this fountain of refreshing streams shall be increased in its richness and plenteousness by anything which he has written. All, or nearly all, love singing. There is music in the souls of all, though all cannot sing. Old Humphrey says, " Though but a poor singer, yet have I a habit of singing when alone. A little thing sets me off—a bit of green on the earth, or a bit of blue in the skies. Yes, yes, I like singing, and often sing with my heart when my lips are silent. I like to hear a milkmaid singing in the green meadow, when her heart is so happy

that she cannot help it.   I love to hear a song
uncalled for.   Who asks the birds to sing?
They sing to relieve their hearts, and this is
the sort of singing that I like.   I love to hear
a loud hallelujah, not by the clear musical voice
of one who is paid for it, but by a thousand
tongues singing with the heart and understanding.   You shall have my favourite song.   I
sang it in my youth, and in my manhood, and
now I am singing it in my years :—

> When all Thy mercies, O my God,
>   My rising soul surveys,
> Transported with the view, I'm lost
>   In wonder, love, and praise."

Some have voices harsh, and broken, and most
unmusical, who, notwithstanding, make melody
within.   Old Thomas Fuller says : " Lord, my
voice by nature is harsh and untunable ; and it
is vain to lavish any art to better it.   Can my
singing of psalms be pleasing to Thy ears, which
is unpleasant to my own ?   Yet, though I cannot
chant with the nightingale, or chirp with the
blackbird, I had rather chatter with the swallow;
yea, rather croak with the raven, than be altogether silent.   Hadst Thou given me a better
voice I would have praised Thee with a better

voice ; now, what my music wants in sweetness, let it have in sense—singing praises with my understanding. Yea, Lord, create in me a new heart, therein to make melody ; and I will be contented with my old voice until in Thy due time, being admitted into the choir of heaven, I have another, more harmonious, bestowed on me."

Whatever singing qualifications we may possess, whether our vocal powers are superior or inferior to others, may there be found in every one of us a heart to praise the Lord, and may the writer and all his readers be assisted in this blessed exercise,

"Till, added to that heavenly choir,
We raise our songs of triumph higher,
    And praise Thee in a bolder strain ;
Out-soar the first born seraph's flight,
And sing, with all our friends in light,
    Thy everlasting love to man."

AMEN.

PRINTED BY R. W. SHARP, BRIGGATE, LEEDS.

www.ingramcontent.com/pod-product-compliance
Lightning Source LLC
Chambersburg PA
CBHW030610270326
41927CB00007B/1106